MAMMALS O

NATIONAL

SOOGDIERE ▮ ▮ MAMMIFERES ▬ SÄUGETIERE

Struik Publishers (Pty) Ltd
(a member of The Struik Publishing Group (Pty) Ltd)
Cornelis Struik House
80 McKenzie Street
Cape Town 8001

Reg.No: 54/00965/07

First published by the National Parks Board, Pretoria
Second edition published by Struik Publishers, 1988
Third edition published by Struik Publishers, 1995

TEXT © Struik Publishers, 1995
PHOTOGRAPHS © individual photographers (see below), 1995
SPOOR DRAWINGS © Louis Liebenberg, from *A Field Guide to the
Animal Tracks of Southern Africa*, David Philip Publishers, 1990.
SYMBOL ILLUSTRATIONS © Chris and Tilde Stuart, from *Southern, Central and
East African Mammals: A Photographic Guide*, Struik Publishers, 1992.
MAP © Struik Publishers, 1995; © in published edition Struik Publishers, 1995.

ENGLISH TEXT: Johan Fourie
AFRIKAANS TRANSLATOR: Johan Fourie
GERMAN TRANSLATOR: Ursula Stevens
GERMAN EDITOR: Bettina Kaufmann
FRENCH TRANSLATOR: Cécile Spottiswoode
IN-HOUSE EDITOR: Ilze Bezuidenhout
DESIGNER: Julie Farquhar

Typesetting by Struik DTP, Cape Town
Reproduced by Unifoto (Pty) Ltd, Cape Town
Printed and bound by CTP Book Printers (Pty) Ltd, PO Box 6060, Parow East 7501

PHOTOGRAPHIC CREDITS: Daryl Balfour - p 47; Daryl Balfour/ABPL - pp 21, 59; Anthony Bannister -
pp 31, 37, 41; Anthony Bannister/ABPL - p 151; Peter Chadwick/ABPL - p 35; Roger de la Harpe -
front cover (bottom right), pp 61, 115; Roger de la Harpe/ABPL - pp 33, 145; Roger de la
Harpe/Natal Parks Board - p 103; Nigel Dennis - pp 29, 53, 89, 93, 123, 147; Nigel Dennis/ABPL -
p 157; Nigel Dennis/SIL - front cover (top left and right; bottom left), pp 1, 11, 13, 43, 49, 55, 63,
67, 69, 71, 81, 85, 87, 97, 101, 109, 113, 119, 129, 131, 133, 137, 139, 141, 149, 153, 155, 159; GPL
du Plessis/Photo Access - p 51; Johan Fourie - p 23; Clem Haagner/ABPL - pp 39, 57, 73, 95; Dave
Hamman/ABPL - p 75; Leonard Hoffmann/SIL - p 135; Robert C. Nunnington/ABPL - pp 77, 111;
Peter Pickford/SIL pp 15, 83, 121; Rob Ponte/ABPL - p 117; Eric Reisinger/ABPL - p 19; Philip
Richardson/ABPL - pp 17, 65; Brendan Ryan/ABPL - p 25; Chris and Tilde Stuart - p 91; Johnathan
Swart - p15; Heinrich van den Berg/HPH Photography - pp 79, 107; Herman van den Berg/HPH
Photography - pp 27, 105; Philip van den Berg/HPH Photography - pp 45, 99, 125, 127, 143.

ISBN 1-86825-726-6

FRONT COVER: *(clockwise from top left)* Giraffe; Zebra; Lion; Gemsbok

CONTENTS

FOREWORD

Several years ago, while on a visit to Tasmania, I presented a photographic book on mammals of the South African national parks to a friend of mine who had immigrated to the island. With tear-filled eyes he admitted, while paging through the book, that what he and his family missed most was the wildlife.

Africa is renowned for its large mammals and South Africa is blessed with a network of national parks conserving all of these found within our boundaries. During your visit to the various national parks your experience will be greatly enriched if you are able to identify most of the common mammals you encounter. It is therefore with sincere gratitude that I thank Struik Publishers for its efforts in revising and updating this booklet which will give much pleasure and make your visit to the national parks of South Africa even more memorable. It will also assist in achieving the National Parks Board's ultimate goal of making the national parks of our country the pride and joy of every South African.

Dr G.A. Robinson
Chief Executive
National Parks Board

VOORWOORD

Etlike jare gelede, terwyl ek Tasmanië besoek het, het ek 'n fotografiese boek oor die soogdiere van Suid-Afrika se nasionale parke aan 'n vriend van my, wat daarheen geïmmigreer het, gegee. Met betraande oë het hy deur die boek geblaai en erken dat hy en sy familie die dierelewe van Suid-Afrika meer as enigiets mis.

Afrika is bekend vir sy groot soogdiere. Suid-Afrika is geseën met 'n netwerk nasionale parke wat die volle verskeidenheid van soogdiere eie aan dié gebied bewaar. Tydens u besoek aan die verskillende nasionale parke sal u belewenis aansienlik verryk word, as u in staat gestel word om die meer algemene soogdiere te kan identifiseer. Daarom wil ek Struik Uitgewers in die besonder bedank vir hul pogings om hierdie boek te hersien en inligting by te werk. Die boek gee u die geleentheid om meer genot uit u besoek aan ons nasionale parke te put en 'n onvergeetlike ervaring daarvan te maak. Dit dra ook by tot die bereiking van die Nasionale Parkeraad se uiteindelike oogmerk, om die nasionale parke van ons land die trots en plesier van elke Suid-Afrikaner te maak.

Dr G.A. Robinson
Hoof Uitvoerende Direkteur
Nasionale Parkeraad

AVANT-PROPOS

Lors d'une visite en Tasmanie, il y a de cela plusieurs années, j'ai offert à un des mes amis qui avait immigré là-bas, un ouvrage illustré sur les mammifères des parcs nationaux d'Afrique du Sud. Et, tout en feuilletant cet ouvrage, c'est avec des larmes dans les yeux qu'il m'a confié que, ce qui lui manquait le plus à lui et à sa famille, c'était la vie sauvage d'Afrique du Sud. Le continent africain est réputé pour ses grands mammifères et l'Afrique du Sud est doté d'un riche réseau de parcs nationaux qui protègent chaque espèce existant à l'intérieur des frontières du pays. Votre visite de divers parcs nationaux sera une expérience d'autant plus riche si vous êtes en mesure d'identifier la plupart des mammifères que vous apercevrez. C'est donc avec une immense gratitude que je tiens à remercier Struik Publishers pour avoir revu, corrigé et remis à jour cette publication qui rendra d'autant plus mémorable votre séjour dans les parcs nationaux d'Afrique du Sud.

Dr G.A. Robinson
Directeur en chef
Comité des Parcs nationaux

VORWORT

Vor einigen Jahren besuchte ich Tasmanien und überreichte einem guten Freund, der dorthin ausgewandert war, einen Bildband über die Säugetiere in den südafrikanischen Nationalparks. Mit Tränen in den Augen gestand er, daß er und seine Familie die Tiere besonders vermissen würden.

Afrika ist für seine großen Säugetiere bekannt, und Südafrika hat ein besonders breitgefächertes Netzwerk an Naturreservaten und -parks, in denen die Tiere in ihrem natürlichen Lebensraum geschützt werden. Der Besucher benötigt jedoch einen kleinen Führer, um in den verschiedenen Reservaten die Tiere identifizieren und einordnen zu können.

Ich bin daher dem Struik Verlag für die überarbeitete und aktualisierte Auflage dieses Büchleins sehr dankbar, und bin auch davon überzeugt, daß es dem Besucher eine Hilfe sein wird, die Säugetiere zu erkennen. Dadurch hat der Besucher mehr Spaß an einem Besuch in einem der Naturreservate Südafrika, ein Ergeignis, das dem Besucher lange in – guter – Erinnerung bleiben sollte.

Dr G.A. Robinson
Vorstandvorsitzender
National Parks Board

INTRODUCTION

The mission of the National Parks Board of South Africa is to create a system of national parks representative of the diversity of natural systems in South Africa, and to develop them and manage them to the maximum benefit of all visitors, South Africans and foreign tourists.

South Africa has a great diversity of natural habitats. In order to represent all of these veld types in a system of national parks, some 40 national parks should be created. At present the National Parks Board controls 17 areas, representing about three per cent of the land area of the country.

Many of the parks are now in a developing phase. They change continually due to acquisition of new land and the re-establishment of a number of indigenous game species. This means that smaller parks are improving all the time, offering every tourist more and more.

INLEIDING

Die missie van die Nasionale Parkeraad is om 'n landwye stelsel van nasionale parke te skep, verteenwoordigend van die diversiteit van natuurstelsels in Suid-Afrika. Die Parkeraad moet hierdie parke dan ook ontwikkel en bestuur sodat Suid-Afrikaanse en buitelandse besoekers die grootste voordeel daaruit kan trek.

Suid-Afrika het 'n groot verskeidenheid natuurlike habitatte – Acocks het nie minder nie as 70 verskillende veldtipes geïdentifiseer. Ten einde al hierdie veldtipes in 'n nasionale parkstelsel te verteenwoordig, sal sowat 40 parke geskep moet word. Tans beheer die Nasionale Parkeraad sewentien gebiede, wat ongeveer 3% van die land se oppervlak uitmaak.

Baie parke is nog in 'n ontwikkelende stadium, en verander gedurig weens die aankoop van nuwe grond en die hervestiging van inheemse wildspesies. Dit beteken dat die kleiner parke voortdurend verbeter word.

INTRODUCTION

Le Comité des Parcs nationaux d'Afrique du Sud a pour but de créer un réseau de parcs nationaux qui soit représentatif de la diversité des écosystèmes du pays, de les développer et de les gérer, de façon à ce que les visiteurs sud-africains et étrangers en tirent un maximum de profit. L'Afrique du Sud offre un grand éventail d'habitats naturels. Pour être en mesure de représenter toute la gamme de divers types de veld du pays, il faudrait créer une quarantaine de parcs nationaux. Il y a 17 régions, ce qui représente environ 3% de la superficie du pays.

De nombreux parcs sont en cours de développement et l'acquisition constante de nouveaux territoires ainsi que la réintroduction de la faune dans son habitat d'origine modifient continuellement leur superficie. De ce fait, les parcs les moins grands sont en continuelle mutation et offrent au touriste de plus en plus d'attraits.

EINLEITUNG

Die Aufgabe des National Parks Board von Südafrika besteht darin, landweit ein Netzwerk von Naturschutzgebieten zu schaffen, die die Vielfalt der Biome widerspiegeln, und sie zum größtmöglichen Nutzen aller in- und ausländischen Besucher zu entwickeln und verwalten.

Südafrika besitzt wirklich viele natürliche Habitats. Um sie alle zu repräsentieren, müssten etwa 40 Naturschutzgebiete entwickelt werden. Gegenwärtig kontrolliert der Parks Board 17 Gebiete, was etwa 3% der Landesoberfläche entspricht.

Viele Wildparks befinden sich in einer Entwicklungsphase. Durch Landankauf und Wiedereinführung einheimischer Wildspezien, verändern sie sich ständig. Dies bedeutet, daß kleineren Naturschutzgebiete sich stetig verbessern, und dem Besucher mehr und mehr bieten.

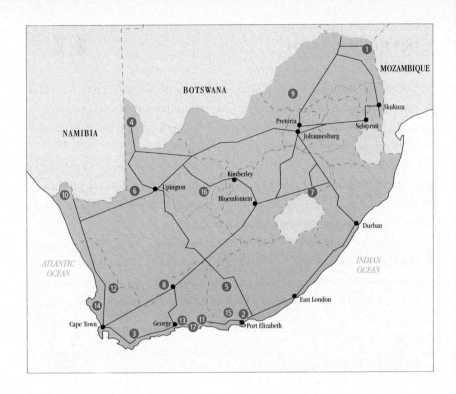

1. Kruger National Park

2. Addo Elephant National Park

3. Bontebok National Park

4. Kalahari Gemsbok
   National Park

5. Mountain Zebra National Park

6. Augrabies Falls National Park

7. Golden Gate Highlands
   National Park

8. Karoo National Park

9. Marakele National Park

10. Richtersveld National Park

11. Tsitsikamma National Park

12. Tankwa Karoo National Park

13. Wilderness National Park

14. West Coast National Park

15. Zuurberg National Park

16. \Hei-!gariep National Park

17. Knysna National Lake Area

Key to symbols/Simboolsleutel/Symbolerklärung/Légende

♀	FEMALE/VROULIK/WEIBLICH/FEMELLE
♂	MALE/MANLIK/MÄNNLICH/MÂLE
	LENGTH (INCLUDING TAIL)/LENGTE (MET STERT)/LÄNGE (SCHWANZ INKLUSIVE)/LONGUEUR (AVEC LA QUEUE)
	LENGTH (EXCLUDING TAIL)/LENGTE (SONDER STERT)/LÄNGE (OHNE SCHWANZ)/LONGUEUR (SANS QUEUE)
	HEIGHT/HOOGTE/GRÖSSE/HAUTEUR
	HEIGHT AT SHOULDER/SKOUERHOOGTE/ SCHULTERHÖHE/HAUTEUR JUSQU'AUX ÉPAULES
	SPEED/SPOED/GESCHWINDIGKEIT/VITESSE
	RECORD HORN LENGTH/REKORD HORINGLENGTE/DIE LÄNGSTEN HÖRNER/RECORD DE LONGUEUR DES CORNES
	RIGHT FRONT PAW/REGTER VOORPOOT/RECHTE VORDERPFOTE/PATTE D'AVANT DROITE
KRUGER, BONTEBOK, KAROO	NATIONAL PARKS WHERE MAMMAL CAN BE FOUND/NASIONALE PARKE WAAR SOOGDIER AANGETREF WORD/NATIONAL PARKS, IN DENEN SÄUGETIERE LEBEN/DES PARCS NATIONAUX OÙ ON PEUT TROUVER DES MAMMIFERES

Papio ursinus

CHACMA BABOON

Widespread in many national parks, these are social animals, occurring in troops of up to 100 individuals. Chacma Baboons are omnivorous and feed on a wide variety of items, from grass seeds and wild fruit to insects, hares and the young of small antelope. There is no fixed mating season and a single young is born after a six-month gestation period. Life expectancy is 45 years.

KAAPSE BOBBEJAAN

Kom algemeen in baie nasionale parke voor. Groeplewend en kom in troppe van tot 100 diere voor. Hulle is omnivore en benut 'n verskeidenheid kossoorte: grassade, veldvrugte, insekte, hase en die lammers van kleiner boksoorte. Daar is geen vaste paringseisoen nie. 'n Enkele kleintjie word gewoonlik gebore na 'n draagtyd van ses maande. Die waarskynlike lewensduur is 45 jaar.

LE BABOUIN CHACMA

Ce babouin est très répandu dans de nombreux parcs nationaux. C'est un animal sociable qui vit en bandes qui peuvent compter jusqu'à une centaine de bêtes. Il est omnivore et se nourrit de toute une gamme d'aliments comprenant aussi bien des graines et des fruits sauvages que des insectes, des lièvres et de jeunes antilopes. Cet animal n'a pas de saison de reproduction fixe et après une période de gestation de six mois, la femelle ne met bas qu'un seul petit.

TSCHAKMA-PAVIAN

Diese geselligen Tiere sind in den Naturschutzgebieten weit verbreitet; sie formieren sich in Gruppen bis zu 100 Tieren. Paviane sind Allesfresser und ihre vielfältige Nahrung schließt Grassamen, Wildfrüchte, Insekten und sogar Antilopenkitze ein. Paviane haben keine feste Paarungszeit. Nach einer Tragzeit von sechs Monaten wird ein Junges geboren. Die Lebens-erwartung dieser Tiere liegt bei 45 Jahren.

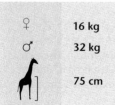

♀   16 kg

♂   32 kg

75 cm

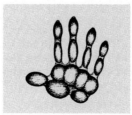

KRUGER, MARAKELE,
AUGRABIES FALLS,
MOUNTAIN ZEBRA,
GOLDEN GATE HIGHLANDS,
KALAHARI GEMSBOK,
ZUURBERG, KAROO,
TANKWA KAROO,
\HEI-!GARIEP, RICHTERSVELD

11

Cercopithecus aethiops

VERVET MONKEY

Common in forested regions, especially along river banks, these are social animals, occurring in groups of 15 to 20 individuals. Vervet Monkeys live mainly on wild fruit, insects, birds' eggs and chicks. They are exclusively diurnal and sleep in trees at night. There is no fixed mating season and a single young is born after a gestation period of seven months. Life expectancy is 24 years.

BLOUAAP

Hierdie diertjie het geen vaste paringseisoen nie. 'n Enkele kleintjie word gebore na 'n draagtyd van sewe maande. Algemeen in bosagtige omgewings, veral langs rivieroewers. Blouape kom voor in klein troppe van 15-20 diere. Hulle kan goed swem. Leef van wilde vrugte, insekte, voëleiers, kuikens of enigiets wat eetbaar is. Die waarskynlike lewensduur is 24 jaar.

LE VERVET

On le trouve surtout dans les régions boisées et en particulier le long des rivières. C'est un animal sociable qui vit en bandes de 15 à 20 individus. Il se nourrit essentiellement de fruits sauvages et d'insectes mais il consomme aussi les oeufs des oiseaux et leurs petits. Cet animal n'a pas de saison de reproduction fixe et après une période de gestation de sept mois, la femelle ne met bas qu'un seul petit. Le vervet peut vivre jusqu'à 24 ans.

GRÜNMEERKATZE

Grünmeerkatzen bevorzugen bewaldete Gegenden, besonders in der Nähe von Flußufern. Sie sind gesellige Tiere, die sich zu Gruppen von 15 bis 20 Tieren zusammenschließen. Ihre Hauptnahrung besteht aus Wildfrüchten, Insekten, Vogeleiern und jungen Vögeln. Es gibt keine bestimmte Paarungszeit, und ein Junges wird nach einer Tragzeit von sieben Monaten geboren. Die Lebenserwartung liegt bei 24 Jahren.

Cercopithecus aethiops

♀ ♂   5 kg

1,15 m

Kruger, Marakele,
Addo Elephant,
Augrabies Falls,
Mountain Zebra,
Zuurberg, Karoo,
Tsitsikamma,
\Hei-!gariep,
Richtersveld

Manis temminckii

PANGOLIN

The upper body is covered with horny scales. Solitary, nocturnal animals, living in holes, Pangolins feed on termites and ants by breaking open the nests with their strong claws and removing the insects with their sticky tongues. When endangered, they roll into a tight ball, head inside. One young is born after a gestation period of 140 days. Life expectancy is 12 years.

IETERMAGÔ

Die hele liggaam, behalwe die onderkant, is met harde horingskubbe bedek. Alleenlopend, hoofsaaklik naglewend en woon in gate. Hulle vreet miere en termiete deur neste met hul sterk kloue oop te grawe, en die insekte met hul taai tonge uit te haal. Wanneer bedreig, rol hy hom in 'n stywe bal op, kop na binne. Een kleintjie word gebore na 'n draagtyd van 140 dae.

LE PANGOLIN

Le haut de son corps est recouvert de grandes écailles cornées et dures et on l'appelle parfois fourmilier à écailles. Le pangolin est un animal solitaire et noc-turne, qui vit dans un terrier. Pour se nourrir, cet animal éventre les termitières et les fourmilières avec ses longues griffes et attrape ses victimes avec sa langue gluante. Généralement, en cas d'alerte, il se roule en boule protégeant ainsi sa tête. La femelle ne met bas qu'un seul petit.

SCHUPPENTIER

Hornartige Schuppen bedecken die obere Körperhälfte dieses Einzelgängers. Das Schuppentier ist nachts aktiv und lebt in Höhlen. Es ernährt sich von Ameisen und Termiten, indem es den Ameisen- oder Termitenbau mit seinen starken Krallen aufbricht und die Insekten mit seiner klebrigen Zunge heraus-zieht. Bei drohender Gefahr rollt es sich zu einem festen Ball zusammen und schützt seinen Kopf in dessen Mitte. Es gebiert nur ein Junges.

14

Manis temminckii

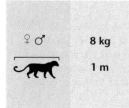

♀♂   8 kg

1 m

KRUGER,
MARAKELE,
AUGRABIES FALLS,
KALAHARI GEMSBOK,
\HEI-!GARIEP

Atelerix frontalis

HEDGEHOG

Nocturnal animals that live in holes or under shelter by day, Hedgehogs come out at night to hunt insects, worms, snails, small mice and lizards; they also take eggs and soft fruit. When endangered, they roll into a small, prickly ball. They usually hibernate in the colder months. Litters average four young and are born in summer, after a gestation period of 35 days.

KRIMPVARKIE

'n Nagdiertjie wat bedags in gate of onder beskutting skuil. Kom teen die aand uit om insekte, wurms, slakke, klein muise, akkedisse, eiers en selfs sagte vrugte soek om te eet. Wanneer bedreig, rol hy homself op in 'n stewige, stekelrige bal. Ondergaan 'n kort winterslaap vanaf Mei tot Julie. Twee tot vier kleintjies word gedurende die somer gebore na 'n draagtyd van 35 dae.

LE HERISSON

C'est un animal nocturne qui se terre pendant la journée. Il sort la nuit pour attraper des insectes, des vers, des escargots, des lézards et des souris; il se nourrit également de fruits. Cet animal préfère les régions herbeuses ou les forêts. En cas de danger, il se roule en boule. En général, il hiberne pendant la saison froide. En été, la femelle met bas en moyenne quatre petits, après une période de gestation de 35 jours.

IGEL

Diese Nachttiere leben in Erdlöchern. Sie ernähren sich von Insekten, Würmern, Schnecken, Mäusen und Eidechsen, gelegentlich auch von Eiern und weichen Früchten. Sie jagen nachts. Wenn Gefahr droht, rollen sie sich zu einem stacheligen Ball zusammen. Die kälteren Monate verbringt der Igel im Winterschlaf. Ein Wurf enthält ungefähr vier Junge, die im Sommer nach einer Tragzeit von 35 Tagen geboren werden.

Atelerix frontalis

 ♀ ♂

350 g

17-22 cm

Kruger,
Mountain Zebra,
Golden Gate Highlands

Lepus capensis

CAPE HARE

Cape Hares prefer open, dry habitat such as grassland, or grassland with sparse scrub. They are nocturnal and solitary. By day they hide in grass or scrub with their ears folded back; they will hide in holes if endangered. Cape Hares emerge after sunset to graze, and feed on short grass. One to three young are born after a gestation period of 42 days. Life expectancy is five to six years.

VLAKHAAS

Vlakhase verkies oop, droë habitat soos grasveld, of grasveld met yl bossies. Hulle is nagdiere en alleenlopend. Bedags skuil hulle met die ore platgevou in gras of bossies. Hulle kruip in gate as hulle bedreig word. Hulle kom na sononder uit om te wei, en leef van gras. Tot drie kleintjies per werpsel word gebore na 'n draagtyd van 42 dae. Die waarskynlike lewensduur is vyf tot ses jaar.

LE LIEVRE DU CAP

Cet animal préfère un habitat découvert tel que la savane herbeuse ou broussailleuse. Il est nocturne et solitaire. Pendant la journée, il se cache dans l'herbe ou sous les broussailles avec ses oreilles rabattues et, s'il se sent menacé, il se terre. Il sort se nourrir à la nuit tombante et mange des herbes courtes. Après une période de gestation de 42 jours, la femelle met bas d'un à trois petits. Le lièvre peut vivre pendant cinq ou six ans.

KAPHASE

Der Kaphase bevorzugt das offene Feld oder spärlich bewachsenes Grasland. Er ist ein Nachttier und Einzelgänger. Tagsüber versteckt er sich im Gras oder Gebüsch; bei Gefahr sucht er in Erdlöchern Schutz. Nach Sonnenuntergang beginnt er zu fressen, wobei er kurzes Gras bevorzugt. Ein bis drei Junge werden nach einer Tragzeit von 42 Tagen geboren. Die Lebenserwartung der Kaphasen liegt bei fünf bis sechs Jahren.

Lepus capensis

 ♀ ♂ 2 kg

45-60 cm

Kruger, Augrabies Falls,
Mountain Zebra,
Bontebok,
Kalahari Gemsbok,
Karoo, Richtersveld,
Tankwa Karoo,
\Hei-!Gariep,
West Coast

Lepus saxatilis

SCRUB HARE

The Scrub Hare is similar to the Cape Hare but favours more densely wooded habitat with shrub cover. Solitary and nocturnal, it lies in a shelter by day with its ears folded back. It emerges in the late afternoon to graze, preferring leaves, stems and rhizomes of green grasses. The Scrub Hare breeds throughout the year; after a gestation period of about 40 days one to three young are born.

KOLHAAS

Die kolhaas verkies 'n meer woudryke habitat met struikgewasse, as die vlak-haas. Hulle is alleenlopend en naglewend, en lê bedags in 'n skuiling, met die ore teruggevou. Hulle kom na sononder uit om te wei, en verkies blare, stingels en wortelstokke van groen gras. Een tot drie kleintjies word dwars-deur die jaar per werpsel gebore na 'n draagtyd van 40 dae.

LE LIEVRE DE BROUSSE

Cette espèce est très proche du lièvre du Cap mais il préfère des terrains plus boisés et broussailleux. Animal solitaire et nocturne, il reste à l'abri pendant la journée avec ses oreilles rabattues. Il sort de son terrier en fin d'après-midi pour aller brouter, de préférence de l'herbe, des tiges et des racines. Le lièvre s'accouple pendant toute l'année. Après une période de gestation de 40 jours, la femelle met bas d'un à trois petits.

STRAUCHHASE

Der Strauchhase ähnelt dem Kaphasen, aber bevorzugt dichter bewachsene Savannen. Er ist ebenfalls ein Einzelgänger und Nachttier. Tagsüber liegt er in Deckung, wo er die Ohren eng an den Kopf legt, um nicht gesehen zu werden. Am Spätnachmittag kommt er dann zum Fressen hervor. Er ernährt sich von Blättern, Grasstengeln und -wurzeln. Ein bis drei Junge werden nach einer Tragzeit von etwa 40 Tagen geboren.

Lepus saxatilis

 ♀ ♂ 3-4 kg
55 cm

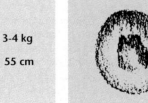

Pronolagus crassicaudatus

NATAL RED ROCK RABBIT

Natal Red Rock Rabbits occur on cliffs and rocky mountain slopes with good grass cover. They are nocturnal and live in small colonies of a few individuals. By day they shelter in rock fissures and thick grass. They are grazers, feeding on grasses and young, green grass blades, mainly in the late afternoon. After a gestation period of one month, one to three young are born.

NATALSE ROOI KLIPKONYN

Hulle kom in die suide van die Krugerwildtuin voor en bewoon kranse en rotsagtige berghange met goeie grasbedekking. Hulle is naglewend en kom in klein kolonies van 'n paar individue voor. Bedags skuil hulle in klipskeure en in dik gras. Hulle is grasvreters wat laatmiddag uitkom om te wei. Een tot drie kleintjies per werpsel word gebore na 'n draagtyd van 'n maand.

LE LIEVRE ROUGE DU NATAL

Ce lièvre peuple les pentes de montagnes rocailleuses. Cet animal est très actif pendant la nuit et vit en petites bandes. Pendant la journée, il s'abrite dans des anfractuosités rocheuses et dans les fourrés. Il est herbivore et sort habituellement en fin d'après-midi pour s'alimenter. C'est un animal très craintif, qui se méfie beaucoup des prédateurs. Après une période de gestation d'un mois, la femelle met bas d'un à trois petits.

ROTES FELSENKANINCHEN

Das Rote Felsenkaninchen lebt auf felsigen Berghängen und grasbewachsenen Felsvorsprüngen. Es ist ein Nachttier. Die Kolonien bestehen aus nur wenigen Hasen. Tagsüber verbergen sich die Felsenkaninchen in Felsspalten und dichtem Gras. Sie sind Grasfresser, die am Spätnachmittag zur Nahrungsaufnahme hervorkommen. Eine Häsin wirft ein bis drei Junge nach einer Tragzeit von einem Monat.

Pronolagus crassicaudatus

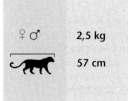

♀♂   2,5 kg

57 cm

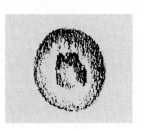

Kruger

Pedetes capensis

SPRINGHARE

Springhares occur on sandy soils in open grassland. They excavate an entrance tunnel to a living chamber, with a smaller escape tunnel. They live on the underground parts and roots of grasses, as well as on stems and seeds above ground. Springhares are nocturnal animals. A single young is born after a 45-day gestation period. Life expectancy is eight years.

SPRINGHAAS

Die springhaas kom op sanderige grond voor. Hulle grawe 'n ingangstonnel na 'n woonvertrek, met 'n kleiner ontsnappingsroete. Hulle leef van die onder-grondse dele en wortels van grasse, asook stingels en sade. Springhase is nag-diere wat na donker uit hul gate kom. 'n Enkele kleintjie word gebore na 'n draagtyd van 45 dae. Hul waarskynlike lewensduur is agt jaar.

LE LIEVRE SAUTEUR

On le trouve dans les régions où il y a des terrains sablonneux. Il creuse une galerie qui débouche sur une chambre et un tunnel de sortie plus petite. Le lièvre se nourrit de la partie souterraine des herbes et des racines et également des tiges et des graines à la surface du sol. C'est un animal nocturne. Après une période de gestation de 45 jours, la femelle ne met bas qu'un seul petit. Cet animal peut vivre pendant sept ou huit ans.

SPRINGHASE

Trotz seines Namens handelt es sich bei diesem Tier um ein Nagetier und nicht um einen Hasen. Die Springhasen bevorzugen sandige Gegenden, die einen Sandboden aufweisen. Sie graben sich einen Eingangs- und Ausgangstunnel zu ihrem Bau. Ihre Nahrung umfaßt Graswurzeln und Grasstengel sowie Samen. Springhasen sind Nachttiere. Ein Junges wird nach einer Tragzeit von 45 Tagen geboren. Die Lebenserwartung liegt bei siebeneinhalb bis acht Jahren.

Pedetes capensis

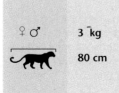

♀ ♂   3 kg

80 cm

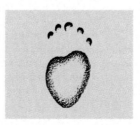

Kruger, Marakele,
Addo Elephant,
Augrabies Falls,
Mountain Zebra,
Golden Gate Highlands,
Kalahari Gemsbok,
Zuurberg, \Hei-!gariep

25

Xerus inauris

GROUND SQUIRREL

Widespread in the drier regions, Ground Squirrels prefer open veld with sparse scrub on hard lime soils. They dig extensive tunnel complexes that accommodate about 30 animals. Their diet consists of insects, plants and seeds, and they also dig for bulbs and tubers. While feeding, the tail is used as an umbrella for shade. One to three young are born after a gestation period of 45 days.

WAAIERSTERTGRONDEEKHORING

Hierdie diertjie kom algemeen in droër dele voor. Hulle verkies oop veld met yl bossies, op harde, kalkagtige grond. Hulle grawe gatkomplekse waarin omtrent 30 diere woon. Hulle vreet insekte, plante, sade en grawe wortels en bolle uit. Terwyl hulle vreet, gebruik hulle die stert as sambreel om 'n skaduwee te gooi. Een tot drie kleintjies word gebore na 'n draagtyd van 45 dae.

L'ECUREUIL TERRESTRE

Très répandu dans les régions sèches, cet écureuil habite les étendues de veld émaillées de broussailles et les sols calcaires. Il creuse un système complexe de galeries souterraines qui abritent jusqu'à une trentaine d'animaux. Il se nourrit d'insectes, de plantes et de graines et déterre des racines et des bulbes. Lorsqu'il mange, sa queue lui sert de parasol. Après une période de gestation de 45 jours, la femelle met bas d'un à trois petits. Cet écureuil peut vivre pendant 15 ans.

ERDHÖRNCHEN

Man trifft sie in trockeneren Gebieten an, da sie offenes, spärlich bewachsenes Grasland und harten, kalkhaltigen Boden bevorzugen. Sie graben ein weitläufiges Tunnelsystem, in dem bis zu 30 Tiere leben können. Ihre Nahrung besteht aus Insekten, Pflanzen und Samen. Beim Fressen dient der Schwanz als schattenspendender Schirm. Sie werfen nach 45 Tagen ein bis drei Junge. Die Lebenserwartung der Tiere liegt bei 15 Jahren.

Xerus inauris

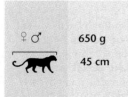

♀ ♂   **650 g**

45 cm

Augrabies Falls,
Mountain Zebra,
Golden Gate Highlands,
Kalahari Gemsbok,
\Hei-!gariep

Paraxerus cepapi

TREE SQUIRREL

An arboreal animal whose diet consists of insects, leaf buds, fruit, seeds and berries, the Tree Squirrel occurs in savanna bushveld, singly or in small family groups. They are dependent on hollow tree trunks for shelter and prefer mopane trees. On detecting danger, they vocalize loudly with a bird-like call. After a gestation period of 55 days, one to three young are born.

BOOMEEKHORING

'n Boomdiertjie wat van insekte, blaarknoppies, vrugte, sade en bessies leef. Hulle is alleenlopend, maar kom ook in klein familiegroepe voor. Hulle kom in die savannabosveld voor, en omdat hulle afhanklik is van hol stamme vir skuiling, is hulle lief vir mopaniebome. Wanneer hulle gevaar bespeur, kwetter hulle luidkeels. Een tot drie kleintjies word gebore na 'n draagtyd van 55 dae.

L'ECUREUIL ARBORICOLE

C'est un animal qui se nourrit d'insectes, de bourgeons, de fruits, de graines et de baies. Il habite la savane broussailleuse et vit seul ou en petits groupes. Il s'abrite dans les troncs d'arbres creux, de préférence ceux des mopanes. S'il se sent menacé, il pousse des cris stridents qui rappellent ceux de certains oiseaux. Après une période de gestation de 55 jours, la femelle met bas d'un à trois petits. Cet écureuil peut vivre pendant 15 ans.

BAUMHÖRNCHEN

Das Baumhörnchen bevorzugt Savannen, die von Büschen durchwachsen sind. Seine Nahrung besteht aus Insekten, Früchten, Blättern und Samen. Es ist ein Einzelgänger, kann sich aber auch zu kleinen Familiengruppen formieren. Sie suchen Schutz in hohlen Baumstämmen. Wittern sie Gefahr, geben sie einen raselnden Ruf von sich. Nach einer Tragzeit von 55 Tagen werden ein bis drei Junge geboren. Die Lebenswerwartung liegt bei 15 Jahren.

Paraxerus cepapi

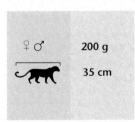

♀ ♂ 200 g

35 cm

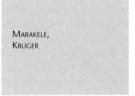

MARAKELE,
KRUGER

29

Hystrix africaeaustralis

PORCUPINE

The Porcupine is nocturnal. The back and hindquarters are protected by hard, sharply pointed quills. These rodents are seen singly or in pairs. By day they shelter in holes or caves, and a few animals may share a shelter. They feed mainly on bark, roots and bulbs, but regularly chew old bones to obtain minerals. After a gestation period of two months, one to four young are born.

YSTERVARK

Die ystervark is 'n nagtelike knaagdier. Hulle beskerm hulself met die skerp, harde penne op hul rug en agterlyf. Hoewel alleenlopend, word pare soms gesien. Bedags skuil hulle in gate of grotte, en 'n paar ystervarke kan so 'n skuiling deel. Hulle vreet hoofsaaklik bas, wortels en knolle, maar knaag ook aan ou bene. Een tot vier kleintjies word gebore na 'n draagtyd van twee maande.

LE PORC-EPIC

Le porc-épic est un animal nocturne. Son dos et son arrière-train sont recouverts de piquants longs et acérés. Ce rongeur vit seul ou en couple. Pendant la journée, il s'abrite dans des trous ou terriers qu'il partage avec d'autres. Il se nourrit surtout d'écorce, de racines et de bulbes mais on sait qu'il mange aussi ce qui reste sur les carcasses. Après une période de gestation de deux mois, la femelle met bas d'un à quatre petits. Il peut vivre pendant 20 ans.

STACHELSCHWEIN

Das Stachelschwein ist ein Nachttier. Scharfe, harte Borsten schützen den Rücken dieses Nagetieres. Den Einzelgänger kann man manchmal auch paarweise antreffen. Tagsüber suchen sie Schutz in Erdlöchern und Höhlen. Sie leben hauptsächlich von Rinde, Wurzeln und Knollen, ab und an auch von Aas. Nach zweimonatiger Tragzeit werden ein bis vier Junge geboren. Die Lebenserwartung der Stachelschweine liegt bei 20 Jahren.

Hystrix africaeaustralis

 ♀ ♂ 17 kg

73-100 cm

ALL PARKS
ALLE PARKE
TOUTES LES RESERVES
ALLE RESERVATE

31

Aonyx capensis

CAPE CLAWLESS OTTER

Found along permanent streams and ponds, as well as in the intertidal zone on the coast and in wetlands, Cape Clawless Otters are diurnal and nocturnal, and feed on crabs, fish, frogs, birds and birds' eggs. They are often seen playing in river rapids. After a nine-week gestation period, a litter of two to five young is born. Life expectancy is 16 years.

GROOTOTTER

Word in standhoudende strome en kuile aangetref, asook in die tussengetysone langs die kus, en by vleilande. Groototters is dag- en naglewend en leef van krappe, vis, paddas, voëls en voëleiers. Hulle word dikwels gesien as hulle in rivier-stroomversnellings speel. Werpsels bestaan uit twee tot vyf kleintjies wat na 'n draagtyd van nege weke gebore word. Hul waarskynlike lewensduur is 16 jaar.

LA LOUTRE A JOUES BLANCHES

On trouve cette loutre le long des rivières pérennes, sur la zone intertidale côtière et dans les régions de marais. A la fois diurne et nocturne, cet animal se nourrit de crabes, de poissons, de grenouilles, et consomme aussi des oiseaux et leurs oeufs. On la voit souvent évoluer dans les torrents. Après une période de gestation de neuf mois, la femelle met bas une portée de deux à cinq petits. La loutre à joues blanches peut vivre pendant 16 ans.

KAPFINGEROTTER

Er lebt in Flüssen, in Teichen, Gezeitenzonen an der Küste und in Schwemm-landgebieten. Der Kapfingerotter ist ein Tag- und Nachttier, ruht sich bei zu großer Hitze aber gerne im Schatten aus. Seine Nahrung besteht aus Krabben, Fischen, Fröschen, Vögeln und Vogeleiern. Sie spielen gern in den Stromschnel-len. Nach einer neunwöchiger Tragzeit werfen sie zwei bis fünf Junge. Ihre Lebenserwartung liegt bei 16 Jahren.

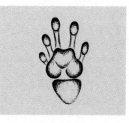

♀ ♂   12 kg

🐾   1,35 m

KRUGER, MARAKELE,
AUGRABIES FALLS, BONTEBOK,
GOLDEN GATE HIGHLANDS,
KAROO, KNYSNA NATIONAL
LAKE AREA, RICHTERSVELD,
TSITSIKAMMA, \HEI-!GARIEP,
WILDERNESS, WEST COAST

33

Mellivora capensis

HONEY BADGER

Mainly nocturnal but also seen in the daytime, these carnivores are fearless and very tough, even attacking Lions. They eat reptiles, birds, small mammals and invertebrates such as baboon spiders and dung-beetle larvae. They are fond of honey and obtain this by cooperating with Honeyguides. One to four young are born after a six-month gestation period. Life expectancy is 24 years.

RATEL

Die ratel is hoofsaaklik naglewend, maar word ook bedags gesien. Hulle is vreesloos en baie taai, en val selfs leeus aan. Hulle vreet reptiele, voëls, klein soogdiere en ongewerweldes soos bobbejaanspinnekoppe en miskruierlarwes. Hulle is lief vir heuning, wat hulle kry word deur saam te werk met die heuning-wyser. Een tot vier kleintjies word gebore na 'n draagtyd van ses maande.

LE RATEL

C'est un animal essentiellement nocturne, bien qu'on l'aperçoive parfois pendant la journée. Le ratel est un carnivore intrépide à qui il arrive même d'attaquer les lions. L'animal se nourrit de reptiles, d'oiseaux, de petits mammifères et d'invertébrés tels que les araignées et les larves des bousiers. Après une période de gestation de six mois, la femelle met bas d'un à quatre petits. Le ratel peut vivre pendant 24 ans.

HONIGDACHS

Diese Fleischfresser sind vorwiegend nachts aktiv, werden aber auch tagsüber gesehen. Bekannt als furchtlose und aggressive Tiere, greifen sie sogar Löwen an. Beim Laufen strecken sie immer den Schwanz hoch. Sie fressen Nagetiere, Vögel, kleine Säugetiere und wirbellose Tiere wie Spinnen und Mistkäfer. Ein bis vier Junge werden nach sechsmonatiger Tragzeit geboren. Die Lebenserwartung der Dachse liegt bei 24 Jahren.

Mellivora capensis

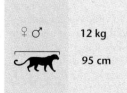

♀ ♂ 12 kg

95 cm

Marakele, Kruger,
Addo Elephant,
Augrabies Falls,
Golden Gate Highlands,
Kalahari Gemsbok,
Zuurberg, Karoo, Tankwa
Karoo, Tsitsikamma,
\Hei-!Gariep, Mountain
Zebra, Wilderness

Ictonyx striatus

STRIPED POLECAT

Striped Polecats are essentially nocturnal and well known for the foul-smelling liquid which is emitted from the anal glands and sprayed in defence. Insects and rodents are the main prey items but these animals also take frogs, birds' eggs and snakes. After a 36-day gestation period, two or three hairless young are born, with eyes and ears closed. Life expectancy is 15 years.

STINKMUISHOND

Die stinkmuishond is hoofsaaklik 'n nagdier. Hulle is bekend vir die onwelriek-ende vloeistof wat uit die anaalkliere gespuit word om vyande af te weer. Hulle vang veral insekte en muise, maar vreet ook paddas, voëleiers en slange. Na 'n draagtyd van 36 dae word twee tot drie haarlose kleintjies gebore met toe oë en ore. Hul waarskynlike lewensduur is 15 jaar.

LE PUTOIS RAYE

Cet animal est essentiellement nocturne. Il est bien connu pour le liquide malo-dorant qu'il sécrète lorsqu'il se sent en danger et qui provient des glandes anales. Il se nourrit surtout d'insectes et de rongeurs mais attrape également des grenouilles, des oeufs d'oiseaux et des serpents. Après une gestation de 36 jours, la femelle met bas deux ou trois petits putois chauves dont les yeux et les oreilles sont fermés. Ce putois peut vivre pendant 15 ans.

STREIFENILTIS

Der Streifeniltis, auch Zorilla genannt, hat ein schwarzes Fell mit vier auffallen-den weißen Streifen. Das Tier ist hauptsächlich in der Nacht aktiv und bekannt für seine ekelerregende Flüssigkeit, die es zur Verteidigung aus seinen Steißdrüsen verspritzt. Zu seiner Beute zählen Insekten, Nagetiere, Frösche, Vogeleier und Schlangen. Zwei oder drei Junge kommen mit geschlossenen Augen nach einer Tragzeit von 36 Tagen zur Welt. Die Lebenserwartung liegt bei 15 Jahren.

Ictonyx striatus

 ♀ ♂   1 kg

62 cm

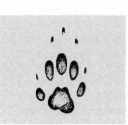

ALL PARKS
ALLE PARKE
TOUTES LES RESERVES
ALLE RESERVATE

Mungos mungo

BANDED MONGOOSE

These social animals occur in groups of five to 30 individuals, usually in rocky habitats. They feed on insects, lizards, birds and small mammals. The 10 to 12 black bars across the back are characteristic. They often hunt with Baboons for insects. Litters of up to eight young are born after a two-month gestation period. Life expectancy is 13 years.

GEBANDE MUISHOND

'n Sosiale diertjie wat in groot troppe van vyf tot 30 diere aangetref word, veral in klipperige omgewings. Hulle vreet insekte, akkedisse, voëls en soogdiertjies. Die 10 tot 12 dwarsstrepe oor die rug is kenmerkend van hierdie diertjie. Jag dikwels saam met bobbejane op soek na insekte. Werpsels van tot agt kleintjies word gebore na 'n draagtyd van 60 dae. Hul waarskynlike lewensduur is 13 jaar.

LA MANGOUSTE ZEBREE

Animal grégaire, la mangouste zébrée se déplace en groupes de cinq à 30 indi-vidus, habituellement dans un habitat rocheux. Elle se nourrit d'insectes, de lézards, d'oiseaux et de petits mammifères. On la reconnaît aux 10 à 12 rayures noires transversales de son dos. Elle chasse souvent les insectes en compagnie des babouins. Après deux mois de gestation, la femelle met bas une portée de huit petits au maximum. Cette mangouste peut vivre pendant 13 ans.

ZEBRAMANGUSTE

Die Kolonien dieser geselligen Tiere mit ihren charakteristischen 10 bis 12 Querstreifen umfassen fünf bis 30 Tiere. Sie lieben felsige Gegenden und ernäh-ren sich von Insekten, Eidechsen, Vögeln und kleinen Säugetieren. Sie jagen oft mit Pavianen nach Insekten. Sie werfen bis zu acht Jungen nach einer zwei-monatigen Tragzeit. Die Kleinen werden von einem der Weibchen, d.h. nicht unbedingt dem Muttertier, gesaugt. Die Lebenserwartung liegt bei 13 Jahren.

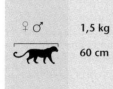

♀ ♂   1,5 kg

60 cm

MARAKELE,
KRUGER

39

Atilax paludinosus

WATER MONGOOSE

The Water Mongoose is uniformly dark brown, and lives among reeds and water plants associated with dams, rivers and wetlands. It is solitary and flees into the water when threatened. It feeds on fish, frogs, crabs, insects, snakes, birds and eggs. Dry crab carapaces often indicate the presence of this animal. One to three young are born between August and September.

KOMMETJIEGATMUISHOND

Leef tussen riete en plante langs riviere, damme en vleilande. Donkerbruin van kleur. Hulle is alleenlopend en vlug die water in as hulle agtervolg word. Hulle vang vis, paddas, krappe, insekte, slange, voëls en vreet graag eiers. Droë doppe van krappe verraai die teenwoordigheid van kommetjiegatmuishonde. Een tot drie kleintjies per werpsel word tussen Augustus en Desember gebore.

LA MANGOUSTE AQUATIQUE

Généralement de couleur brun foncé, cette mangouste vit dans les roseaux ainsi que près des rivières, des étangs et des marais. De nature solitaire, elle se précipite dans l'eau à la moindre alerte. Elle se nourrit de poissons, de grenouilles, de crabes, d'insectes, de serpents, d'oiseaux et d'oeufs. La présence de carapaces de crabes desséchées indique souvent qu'elle est dans les parages. Cette mangouste met bas d'un à trois petits.

WASSERMANGUSTE

Das Fell der Wassermanguste ist dunkelbraun. Sie lebt im Röhricht oder unter Wasserpflanzen in der Nähe von Flüssen, Dämmen und Sümpfen. Bei Gefahr flüchtet dieser Einzelgänger ins Wasser. Zur Nahrung gehören Fische, Frösche, Krabben, Insekten, Schlangen, Vögel und Eier. Trockene Krebsrückenschilder weisen oft auf die Gegenwart dieses Tieres hin. Es werden ein bis drei Junge, meist in der Zeit von August bis Dezember, geboren.

Atilax paludinosus

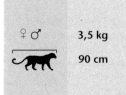 ♀ ♂   3,5 kg

90 cm

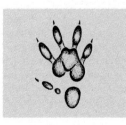

Kruger, Marakele,
Addo Elephant,
Augrabies Falls, Bontebok,
Golden Gate Highlands,
Zuurberg, Karoo, Knysna
National Lake Area,
Richtersveld, Tsitsikamma,
\Hei-!garieb, Mountain Zebra,
West Coast, Wilderness

41

Helogale parvula

DWARF MONGOOSE

These small, dark brown animals are active by day. At night they take shelter in termite mounds or hollow tree trunks. They are social, occurring in groups of 20 or more. They feed on insects, larvae of insects, reptiles and small rodents. While foraging, they maintain contact with sharp, chirpy vocalizations. After a 52-day gestation period, litters of up to four young are born.

DWERGMUISHOND

Hierdie klein, donkerbruin diertjies is bedags aktief. Snags skuil hulle in termietneste of hol boomstompe. Hulle is sosiale diertjies, en kom voor in groepe van 20 of meer. Hulle vreet insekte, larwes van insekte, reptiele en klein knaagdiere. Terwyl hulle jag, hou hulle kontak deur middel van 'n kwetterroep. Vier kleintjies word gebore na 'n draagtyd van 52 dae.

LA MANGOUSTE NAINE

C'est un petit animal au poil brun foncé, actif pendant la journée. La nuit, la mangouste naine s'abrite dans des termitières ou dans des troncs d'arbres creux. Elle est grégaire et vit en communautés d'une vingtaine d'individus. Elle se nourrit d'insectes et de leurs larves, de reptiles et de petits rongeurs. Tout à leurs occupations, ces mangoustes se donnent l'alerte en émettant des cris stridents. Après 52 jours, la femelle met bas une portée de quatre petits au maximum.

ZWERGMANGUSTE

Diese kleinenTiere sind tagsüber aktiv. Nachts suchen sie in Termitenbauten oder hohlen Baumstämmen Schutz. Diese geselligen Mangusten können in Gruppen von über 20 Tieren angetroffen werden. Die Tiere haben eine ausgeprägte Sozialstruktur. Sie leben von Insekten, Larven, kleinen Nagetieren und Reptilien. Beim Furagieren stellen sie durch scharfes Gezirp Kontakt her. Bis zu vier Junge werden nach einer Tragzeit von 52 Tagen geboren.

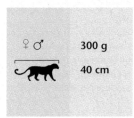

♀ ♂   300 g

40 cm

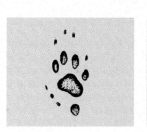

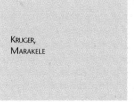

Kruger,
Marakele

Cynictis penicillata

YELLOW MONGOOSE

Widespread in arid inland areas, such as short grassland and semi-desert scrub, these animals feed on insects, scorpions, mice and birds, and are also fond of eggs. Although often seen alone, they may occur in groups of five to 20. They usually dig their own burrows, but will share those of Suricates. They are active during the day. Two to five young are born. Life expectancy is 13 years.

WITKWASMUISHOND

Kom wydverspreid voor in die droër binnelandse gebiede. Hulle vang insekte, skerpioene, muise, voëls en vreet graag eiers. Alhoewel witkwasmuishonde gewoonlik alleen gesien word, woon hulle ook in troppe van vyf tot twintig diere. Hulle is bedags aktief. Gewoonlik word twee (maar tot vyf) kleintjies per werpsel in die somer gebore. Hul waarskynlike lewensduur is 13 jaar.

LA MANGOUSTE JAUNE

Très répandue dans les régions arides de l'intérieur, la mangouste jaune se nourrit d'insectes, de scorpions, de souris et d'oiseaux; elle est aussi friande d'oeufs. La mangouste jaune est un animal qui vit dans la savane. Bien qu'on les voie souvent seules, ces mangoustes se déplacent aussi en groupes de cinq à 20 individus et elles sont diurnes. La femelle met bas de deux à cinq petits. Cet animal peut vivre pendant 13 ans.

FUCHSMANGUSTE

Die weitverbreiteten, am Tag aktiven Fuchsmangusten bevorzugen aride Gegenden. Mangusten ziehen offene, grasbewachsene Steppen vor. Sie leben von Insekten, Skorpionen, Mäusen und Vögeln, aber auch Eier sind sehr beliebt. Obwohl sie Einzelgänger sind, formieren sie sich auch zu Gruppen von fünf bis 20 Tieren. Zwei bis fünf Junge werden geboren. Die Lebenserwartung einer Fuchsmanguste liegt bei 13 Jahren.

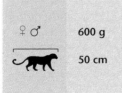

♀ ♂   600 g

50 cm

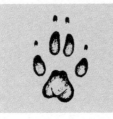

ADDO ELEPHANT,
MOUNTAIN ZEBRA,
BONTEBOK, GOLDEN GATE
HIGHLANDS, KALAHARI
GEMSBOK, ZUURBERG,
KAROO, TANKWA KAROO,
\HEI-!GARIEP, AUGRABIES
FALLS, WEST COAST

Suricata suricatta

SURICATE

Common in the more arid areas of the country, Suricates inhabit a series of holes. They frequently stand erect to survey their surroundings, using their tails for support. They are social animals, occurring in groups of six to 40 animals. Active by day, they feed mainly on insects but also take reptiles and birds. Two or three young are born after a gestation period of 70 days.

STOKSTERTMEERKAT

Kom algemeen in droër binnelandse gebiede voor. Hulle woon in gate en word gewoonlik in groepies van ses tot so veel as 40 aangetref. Sit dikwels soggens in die kenmerkende regop houding voor die gat om warm te word. Hulle is bedags aktief, en vreet hoofsaaklik insekte, maar ook reptiele en voëls. Twee of drie kleintjies word gebore na 'n draagtyd van 70 dae.

LE SURICATE

Très répandu dans les zones arides du pays, le suricate habite une série de terriers devant lesquels il prend un bain de soleil le matin. Il se met debout pour inspecter les environs et se sert de sa queue pour garder l'équilibre. C'est un animal sociable qui vit en groupes comprenant de six à 40 animaux. Diurne, il se nourrit surtout d'insectes mais également d'oiseaux et de reptiles. La femelle met bas deux ou trois petits. Le suricate peut vivre pendant 13 ans.

ERDMÄNNCHEN

Die geselligen Surikate (der Familienname der Erdmännchen) bewohnen die trockenen Gebiete des Landes. Morgens sonnen sie sich vor ihren Bauten, die von vielen Tunneln durchzogen sind. Bis zu 40 Tieren können in einem Bau zusammenleben. Sie stellen sich oft auf ihren Schwanz, um die Umgebung zu beobachten. Sie sind Tagtiere, die sich hauptsächlich von Insekten ernähren, aber auch Reptilien und Vögel fressen. Sie werfen zwei bis drei Junge.

Suricata suricatta

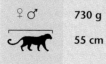

♀ ♂

730 g

55 cm

KALAHARI GEMSBOK,
KAROO,
TANKWA KAROO,
\HEI-!GARIEP,
MOUNTAIN ZEBRA,
AUGRABIES FALLS

Procavia capensis

ROCK DASSIE

Rock Dassies typically seek shelter in rock fissures and among boulders. Because they are hunted by many birds of prey and smaller predators, they never venture too far from their shelters. They are herbivores and active by day. They often climb trees to feed on leaves. After a gestation period of seven-and-a-half months, two or three young are born. Life expectancy is seven years.

KLIPDASSIE

Die klipdassie verkies om in klipskeure en onder rotse te skuil. Hulle is plant-vreters en bedags aktief. Hulle klim dikwels in bome om die blare af te vreet. Omdat hulle gejag word deur verskeie roofvoëls en kleiner roofdiere, waag hulle dit nooit ver van die skuiling nie. Twee of drie kleintjies word gebore na 'n draagtyd van sewe en 'n half maand. Hul waarskynlike lewensduur is sewe jaar.

LE DAMAN DES ROCHERS

Le daman élit domicile dans les anfractuosités rocheuses et entre les gros rochers. Comme il est une proie facile pour les rapaces et d'autres prédateurs, il se risque rarement loin de son abri. C'est un animal herbivore et diurne qui grimpe souvent aux arbres pour se nourrir de feuilles. La femelle met bas deux ou trois petits après une période de gestation de sept mois et demi. Le daman peut vivre pendant sept ans.

KLIPPSCHLIEFER

Es ist typisch für die Klippschliefer, zwischen Felsblöcken Schutz zu suchen. Da sie eine gute Beute für die Raubvögel sind, wagen sie sich nie zu weit von ihrem Schlupfloch weg. Sie sind Vegetarier und tagsüber aktiv. Oft klettern sie auf Bäume, um Blätter zu fressen. Nach einer Tragzeit von siebeneinhalb Monaten werden zwei oder drei Junge geworfen. Die Lebenserwartung der Tiere liegt bei sieben Jahren.

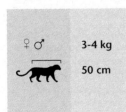

♀ ♂   **3-4 kg**

50 cm

Kruger, Marakele,
Mountain Zebra,
Bontebok, Golden Gate
Highlands, Karoo,
Tsitsikamma, Richtersveld,
Tankwa Karoo,
Augrabies Falls,
West Coast

Vulpes chama

CAPE FOX

A nocturnal animal, feeding mainly on insects, rodents, hares and ground birds, the Cape Fox also scavenges and eats wild fruit. It prefers open grass plains or open scrub veld. It digs its own holes or uses abandoned Springhare holes. The Cape Fox is not social and makes contact only to mate. Three or four young are born after a gestation period of 52 days.

SILWERVOS

'n Nagdiertjie wat veral leef van insekte, muise, hase en grondvoëls. Vreet ook aas en veldvrugte. Verkies oop grasvlaktes of oop bossieveld. Grawe self skuilings, of gebruik gate gemaak deur springhase. Hulle is nie baie sosiaal nie, en maak net kontak om te paar. Drie of vier kleintjies per werpsel word gedurende die lente en somer gebore, na 'n draagtyd van 52 dae.

LE RENARD DU CAP

Le renard du Cap est un animal nocturne. Il se nourrit d'insectes, de petits rongeurs, de lièvres et d'oiseaux qui nichent à même le sol, mais également de charognes et de fruits sauvages. Il préfère les vastes plaines herbeuses ou le veld épineux. Il creuse son propre terrier mais utilise aussi celui du lièvre sauteur lorsqu'il a été abandonné. C'est un animal solitaire qui n'a de contact que pour se reproduire. La femelle met bas trois ou quatre petits après 52 jours.

KAPFUCHS

Der scheue Kapfuchs ist ein Nachttier und ernährt sich hauptsächlich von Insekten, Nagetieren und Vögeln sowie Feldfrüchten, ist aber auch ein Aasfresser. Er bevorzugt offene Grasebenen oder Grasland. Der Kapfuchs gräbt seinen eigenen Bau oder benutzt den verlassenen Bau eines Springhasen. Nur zur Paarung nimmt er zu weiblichen Tieren Kontakt auf. Letztere werfen drei oder vier Junge nach einer Tragzeit von 52 Tagen.

Vulpes chama

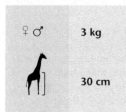

♀ ♂   3 kg

    30 cm

Addo Elephant, Augrabies Falls, Mountain Zebra, Marakele, Bontebok, Golden Gate Highlands, Kalahari Gemsbok, Zuurberg, Karoo, Richtersveld, Tankwa Karoo, \Hei-!gariep, West Coast

Otocyon megalotis

BAT-EARED FOX

These are small, harmless animals living on insects, wild fruit, small rodents and reptiles. They use their large ears to trace sounds of insect activity underground, after which the prey is dug out and eaten. Although they dig their own burrows, they may also move into those dug by other animals. Four to six young are born after a gestation period of two months.

BAKOORVOS

'n Klein skadelose diertjie wat van insekte, veldvrugte, klein knaagdiere en reptiele leef. Hulle groot ore word gebruik om insek-aktiwiteite onder die grond op te spoor, waarna die prooi uitgegrawe en geëet word. Die bakoorvos is bedags en snags aktief. Hulle grawe hul eie skuilings of gebruik erdvarkgate, waar vier tot ses kleintjies na 'n draagtyd van twee maande gebore word.

L'OTOCYON

C'est un petit animal carnivore et inoffensif qui se nourrit généralement d'insectes, de souris, de fruits sauvages et de reptiles. Ses grandes oreilles lui permettent de détecter les bruits souterrains faits par les insectes qu'il déterre pour s'en nourrir. Bien que l'otocyon creuse son propre terrier, il lui arrive aussi d'emprunter celui des autres. La femelle met bas de quatre à six petits après une période de gestation de deux mois.

LÖFFELHUND

Diese kleinen, harmlosen Tiere leben von Insekten, Wildfrüchten, kleinen Nagetieren und Reptilien. Sie leben nicht gerne in hohen Gebiergen oder dichten Wäldern. Mit ihren außergewöhnlich großen, scharfen Ohren nehmen sie unterirdische Geräusche von Insekten wahr, die sie dann ausgraben und fressen. Sie buddeln sich ihren eigenen Bau ebenso wie sie den anderer Tiere übernehmen. Nach zweimonatiger Tragzeit werfen sie vier bis sechs Junge.

Otocyon megalotis

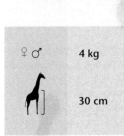

♀ ♂   4 kg

30 cm

Kruger, Addo Elephant,
Augrabies Falls, Mountain
Zebra, Kalahari Gemsbok,
Karoo, Richtersveld,
\Hei-!gariep, West Coast

Canis mesomelas

BLACK-BACKED JACKAL

This predator occurs throughout South Africa and is distinguished by the black 'saddle' with a sprinkling of white hairs on the back. Pairs defend the boundaries of their territory. These efficient hunters capture a variety of prey, including insects, reptiles, scorpions, birds and small mammals; they also scavenge. One to six young are born after a two-month gestation period.

ROOIJAKKALS

'n Roofdier en aasvreter wat dwarsdeur Suid-Afrika voorkom. Word gekenmerk deur 'n swart 'saal' met wit spikkels oor die rug. Hulle is dag- en naglewend. Pare verdedig die grense van hul territoriums. Vang 'n verskeidenheid van prooi soos insekte, reptiele, skerpioene, voëls en klein soogdiere. Werpsels van een tot ses word na 'n draagtyd van twee maande gebore.

LE CHACAL A CHABRAQUE

On trouve ce prédateur dans toute l'Afrique du Sud et on le reconnaît à la 'selle' noire émaillée de poils blancs sur son échine. C'est un animal à la fois diurne et nocturne qui, en couple, défend son territoire. C'est un excellent chasseur et ses proies sont multiples: insectes, reptiles, scorpions, oiseaux et petits rongeurs. C'est également un charognard. La femelle met bas d'un à six petits après une période de gestation de deux mois. Ce chacal peut vivre pendant 10 ans.

SCHABRACKENSCHAKAL

Kennzeichnend ist das schwarze Flankenfell mit einem Anflug von weißen Haaren auf dem Rücken. Sie sind tags wie nachts aktiv und verteidigen in Paaren ihr Territorium. Die Tiere bleiben meist für immer zusammen – sie sind sehr treu. Diese schlauen Jäger erlegen vielerlei Beute: Insekten, Reptilien, Skorpione, Vögel und Säugetiere. Sie sind auch Aasfresser. Nach zweimonatiger Tragzeit werden ein bis sechs Junge geboren. Ihre Lebenserwartung liegt bei zehn Jahren.

Canis mesomelas

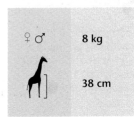

♀ ♂   **8 kg**

38 cm

Kruger, Marakele,
Wilderness, Richtersveld,
Addo Elephant, Augrabies
Falls, Mountain Zebra,
Bontebok, Golden Gate
Highlands, Kalahari
Gemsbok, Zuurberg,
Karoo, Tankwa Karoo,
\Hei-!gariep, West Coast

Canis adustus

SIDE-STRIPED JACKAL

Shy and scarce, Side-striped Jackals feed on small mammals, eggs, insects, ground birds and wild fruit. Their colour is generally grey but at closer range a light-coloured stripe is visible on each flank. The tail has a white tip. They prefer more densely wooded areas than the Black-backed Jackal. Litters of four to six pups are born after a two-month gestation period.

WITKWASJAKKALS

'n Sku en seldsame spesie wat leef van klein soogdiertjies, eiers, insekte, grond-voëls en veldvrugte. Hulle is gryskleurig met 'n duidelike kantstreep en 'n wit kwas op die stert. Nagdiere wat alleen of in pare voorkom. Verkies meer digbe-boste omgewings as die rooijakkals. Werpsels wissel van vier tot ses kleintjies wat na 'n draagtyd van twee maande gebore word.

LE CHACAL A RAYURES LATERALES

C'est un chacal rare et craintif qui se nourrit de petits mammifères, d'oeufs, d'oiseaux terrestres, d'insectes et de fruits sauvages. Son pelage est dans l'ensemble grisâtre mais, vu de plus près, on distingue une rayure caractéris-tique le long de ses flancs. L'extrémité de sa queue est blanche. Contrairement au chacal à chabraque, il se tient dans les régions très boisées. La femelle met bas de quatre à six petits après une période de gestation de deux mois.

STREIFENSCHAKAL

Der scheue und seltene Streifenschakal lebt von kleinen Säugetieren, Eiern, Insekten, Vögeln und Wildfrüchten. Sein Fell ist im allgemeinen grau, und von nahem kann man einen helleren Flankenstreifen sehen. Der Schwanz endet in einer weißen Spitze. Dieser Schakal bevorzugt dichtes Buschwerk. Er ist ruhiger als der Schabrakenschakal. Ein Wurf von vier bis sechs Jungen wird nach einer Tragzeit von zwei Monaten geboren.

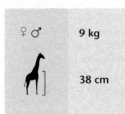

♀ ♂   9 kg

38 cm

Kruger

Lycaon pictus

WILD DOG

The rarest large carnivores of the subregion, Wild Dogs are social hunters of the open plains and savanna woodland, and occur in groups of ten to 15 animals. They pursue a herd of prey animals and single one out, chasing and attacking it until it succumbs. They will often aggressively chase Hyaenas. Seven to ten pups are born after a gestation period of 70 days. Life expectancy is ten years.

WILDEHOND

Die wildehond is 'n sosiale jagter wat in groepe van tien tot 15 voorkom. Hulle jaag gewoonlik 'n trop prooidiere totdat een dier uitgesonder word. Die honde hardloop langs die dier, en val hom aan, totdat hy inmekaarsak, en verskeur hom dan. Wildehonde verjaag hiëna's dikwels op aggressiewe wyse. Sewe tot tien kleintjies word gebore na 'n draagtyd van 70 dae.

LE LYCAON

Les lycaons chassent en meutes qui comptent généralement de 10 à 15 animaux mais qui peuvent atteindre jusqu'à une centaine d'individus. Généralement, ils donnent la chasse à tout un troupeau pour s'acharner ensuite sur un seul d'entre eux qu'ils achèvent. Ils ne craignent pas les hyènes qu'ils attaquent sauvagement. La femelle met bas de sept à huit petits après une période de gestation de 70 jours. Le lycaon peut vivre pendant 10 ans.

HYÄNENHUND

Er ist der größte Hund Afrikas. Dieser gesellige Jäger formiert sich in Gruppen bis zu 100 Tieren, obwohl Meuten von 10 bis 15 Hunden die Norm sind. Sie jagen Tierherden; erwählen ihre Beute, die sie so lange verfolgen, bis diese erschöpft zusammenbricht. Oft hetzen sie sogar auf aggressive Art Hyänen. Sieben bis zehn Junge werden nach einer Tragzeit von 70 Tagen geboren. Ihre Lebenserwartung liegt bei zehn Jahren.

Lycaon pictus

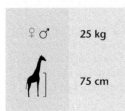

♀ ♂   25 kg

75 cm

KRUGER,
KALAHARI GEMSBOK

59

Crocuta crocuta

SPOTTED HYAENA

The Spotted Hyaena is the larger of the two Hyaena species. Although mainly nocturnal, it is also active by day. Spotted Hyaenas usually live in family groups or 'clans', led by a female. They often scavenge, sometimes even chasing Lion off a kill, but are very capable hunters. One to four pups are born after a three-and-a-half-month gestation period. Life expectancy is 25 years.

GEVLEKTE HIëNA

Die gevlekte hiëna is die grootste van die twee hiënasoorte. Hoewel meer naglewend, is hulle bedags ook aktief. Hulle leef gewoonlik in familiegroepe onder leiding van 'n wyfie. Hulle aas dikwels, maar is ook baie goeie jagters. Verjaag soms leeus van vangste. Een tot vier kleintjies word gebore na 'n draag-tyd van drie en 'n half maand. Hul waarskynlike lewensduur is 25 jaar.

LA HYENE TACHETEE

C'est la plus grande des deux espèces d'hyènes et, bien qu'elle soit surtout nocturne, il est fréquent de la voir aussi pendant la journée. Elle se nourrit habituellement de charognes mais également de proies qu'elle tue elle-même; parfois elle s'attaque même aux lions. La femelle met bas généralement d'un à trois petits après une période de gestation de trois mois et demi. Cet animal peut vivre pendant 25 ans.

FLECKENHYÄNE

Die Fleckenhyäne ist die größere der zwei Hyänenarten. Sie ist zwar hauptsäch-lich nachts aktiv, kann aber auch tagsüber unterwegs sein. Sie leben in Familiengruppen. Diese Tiere sind Aasfresser, doch gleichzeitig auch kluge Jäger. Sie vermögen sogar Löwen von ihrer Beute abzubringen. Ein bis drei Junge werden nach einer dreieinhalbmonatigen Tragzeit geboren. Die Lebens-erwartung der Tiere liegt bei 25 Jahren.

Crocuta crocuta

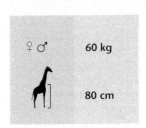

♀ ♂   60 kg

80 cm

Kruger,
Kalahari Gemsbok

Hyaena brunnea

BROWN HYAENA

Scavenging, nocturnal animals, Brown Hyaenas prefer the drier areas of the country. They are usually solitary but may form groups, the size of which varies from five to 14. They are poor hunters and often eat eggs, wild fruit, pods of *acacia* species and insects. After a gestation period of three months, two or three pups are born and raised in a den. Life expectancy is 24 years.

BRUIN HIËNA

'n Aasvretende nagdier wat veral in die droër landstreke voorkom. Hulle is nie afhanklik van water nie. Groepgrootte wissel van vyf tot 14. Hulle is swak jagters, en leef veral van aas. Vreet dikwels eiers, asook veldvrugte, insekte en peule van acacia's. Twee of drie kleintjies word gebore na 'n draagtyd van drie maande en grootgemaak in erdvarkgate. Hul waarskynlike lewensduur is 24 jaar.

LA HYENE BRUNE

C'est un animal nocturne qui se nourrit de charognes. Elle préfère les régions sèches du pays. La taille du groupe varie entre cinq et 14 bêtes. C'est un piètre chasseur et elle s'alimente d'oeufs, de fruits sauvages, de gousses d'acacias et d'insectes. Après une période de gestation de trois mois, la femelle met bas de deux à trois petits qu'elle élève dans sa tanière. La hyène brune peut vivre pendant 24 ans.

BRAUNE HYÄNE

Die Braune Hyäne ist ein Aasfresser und Nachttier. Sie bevorzugt die trockenen Gebiete des Landes. Die Meuten zählen fünf bis 14 Tiere. Die Braune Hyäne ist ein schlechter Jäger und frißt deshalb oft Eier, Wildfrüchte, Schoten der Akazien und Insekten. Die Hyäne ist überwiegend nachts aktiv. Nach dreimonatiger Tragzeit wirft das Weibchen ein oder zwei Junge, die sie anfangs im Bau großzieht. Die Lebenserwartung der Tiere liegt bei 24 Jahren.

Hyaena brunnea

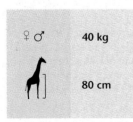

♀ ♂   **40 kg**

    80 cm

MARAKELE,
KRUGER,
AUGRABIES FALLS,
KALAHARI GEMSBOK,
RICHTERSVELD,
\HEI-!GARIEP

Proteles cristatus

AARDWOLF

Aardwolfs live mainly on termites, but also eat moths, spiders, ants and other insects; due to their small, weak teeth they are not capable of dealing with larger prey. They are nocturnal, often hiding in Aardvark holes in the daytime; Aardwolfs are competent diggers and also excavate their own burrows. Two to four young are born after a two-month gestation period.

MAANHAARJAKKALS

Leef hoofsaaklik van termiete, maar vreet ook motte, spinnekoppe, miere en ander insekte. Hulle tande is klein en swak, derhalwe kan hulle nie groter prooi vreet nie. Naglewend en skuil bedags in erdvarkgate. Hulle is goeie grawers en sal soms self gate vergroot. Wanneer bedreig, staan die hare op die rug regop. Twee tot vier kleintjies word na 'n draagtyd van twee maande gebore.

LE PROTELE

Cet animal se nourrit surtout de termites, mais il chasse aussi des phalènes, des araignées et d'autres insectes. Ses dents sont trop petites pour lui permettre de s'attaquer à des proies plus grandes. Le protèle est nocturne et a tendance à s'abriter dans le gîte de l'oryctérope pendant la journée. Le protèle sait creuser sa propre tanière. Quand il se sent en danger, les poils de son dos se hérissent. La femelle met bas de deux à quatre petits après deux mois de gestation.

ERDWOLF

Die Hauptnahrung der Erdwölfe sind Termiten, aber sie fressen auch Motten, Spinnen, Ameisen und andere Insekten. Da ihre Zähne klein und schwach sind, machen sie keine Jagd auf große Beute; der Erdwolf ist ein harmloser Fleisch-fresser. Sie sind nachts aktiv. Als gute Gräber buddeln sie ihren eigenen Bau. Droht ihnen Gefahr, stellt sich ihr Rückenhaar auf. Nach zweimonatiger Trag-zeit werfen sie zwei bis vier Junge.

Proteles cristatus

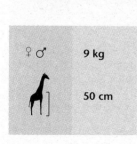

♀♂ 9 kg

50 cm

ALL PARKS
ALLE PARKE
TOUTES LES RESERVES
ALLE RESERVATE

Genetta genetta

SMALL-SPOTTED GENET

This animal resembles the Large-spotted Genet but can be distinguished by its off-white to grey colour and its white-tipped tail. These agile tree climbers are nocturnal and hide by day in trees, hollow trunks or holes in the ground. They feed on small reptiles, insects, small mammals and birds, and also take eggs from nests. Usually three young are born after a gestation period of 70 days.

KLEINKOLMUSKEJAATKAT

Verskil van die grootkolmuskejaatkat op grond van die kleiner kolle en die wit stertpunt. Hulle is naglewend en ratse boomklimmers. Waar bome skaars is, skuil hulle bedags in hol stamme of gate in die grond. Hulle vang klein reptiele, insekte, soogdiere, voëls en verwyder kuikens uit neste. Drie kleintjies word gebore na 'n draagtyd van 70 dae. Hul waarskynlike lewensduur is 13 jaar.

LA GENETTE COMMUNE

Elle ressemble à la genette à grandes taches mais s'en distingue cependant par son pelage d'un blanc grisâtre et par le blanc du bout de sa queue. Grimpeur agile, cet animal nocturne se cache dans les arbres ou dans des trous à même le sol pendant la journée. La genette commune se nourrit de petits reptiles, d'insectes, de mammifères de petite taille, d'oiseaux et aussi d'oeufs. Elle donne le jour à trois petits. La genette commune peut vivre pendant 13 ans.

KLEINFLECKENGINSTERKATZE

Dieses Tier ähnelt der Großfleckginsterkatze, unterscheidet sich aber von dieser durch seins weißlichgraues Fell und seine weiße Schwanzspitze. Die Tiere sind behende Baumkletterer, die sich tagsüber in Bäumen, hohlen Stämmen oder Löchern verbergen. Sie leben von Reptilien, Säugetieren, Vögeln, und Vogel-eiern. Ungefähr drei Junge werden geboren. Die Lebenserwartung dieser Katzen liegt bei 13 Jahren.

 ♀ ♂ 2 kg

95 cm

ALL PARKS
ALLE PARKE
TOUTES LES RESERVES
ALLE RESERVATE

Genetta tigrina

LARGE-SPOTTED GENET

A nocturnal predator preferring dry savanna areas with surface water, the Large-spotted Genet hides in holes or dense trees by day. Large-spotted Genets are fond of rats and mice, but also feed on reptiles, insects, birds and wild fruit. Three to five young are born after a gestation period of two-and-a-half months. Life expectancy is approximately eight years.

GROOTKOLMUSKEJAATKAT

Hierdie nagdier verkies droë savannegebied met oppervlakwater. Die grootkol-muskejaatkat het 'n voorliefde vir rotte en muise, maar vreet ook reptiele, insekte, voëls en veldvrugte. Bedags skuil hulle in digte bome of gate. Drie tot vyf kleintjies word gebore na 'n draagtyd van twee en 'n half maand. Hul waarskynlike lewensduur is ongeveer agt jaar.

LA GENETTE A GRANDES TACHES

C'est un prédateur nocturne qui habite les régions de savane sèche à proximité de points d'eau. La genette à grandes taches se cache dans des trous ou dans des arbres au feuillage épais pendant la journée. Quoiqu'elle aime les rats et les souris, elle se nourrit aussi de reptiles, d'insectes, d'oiseaux et de fruits sauvages. Elle se distingue de la genette commune par de grandes taches d'un brun roux et par sa queue dont le bout est noir. La femelle met bas de trois à cinq petits.

GROSSFLECKENGINSTERKATZE

Dieses nächtliche Raubtier bevorzugt trockene Savanne, und es sucht tagsüber Schutz in Höhlen oder Bäumen. Sie fressen gerne Ratten und Mäuse, Reptilien, Insekten, Vögel und Wildfrüchte. Das Tier hebt sich von der Kleinfleckginster-katze durch seine größeren, rötlichbrauen Flecken und seine schwarze Schwanzspitze ab. Drei bis fünf Junge werden geboren. Die Lebenserwartung der Katzen liegt bei acht Jahren.

Genetta tigrina

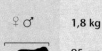 ♀ ♂   1,8 kg

95 cm

KRUGER, MARAKELE,
ADDO ELEPHANT,
BONTEBOK, ZUURBERG,
KNYSNA NATIONAL LAKE
AREA, TSITSIKAMMA,
WILDERNESS,
WEST COAST

CIVET

Civets have a characteristic ridge of dark hair along the spine. The legs are black, and the tail is banded black and white. They mark their routes with secretions from the anal glands; these secretions were used in the past in the manufacturing of perfume. Civets are nocturnal and feed on insects, reptiles, small mammals and wild fruit. After a nine-week gestation period, two to four young are born.

SIWET

Siwette is nagdiere met 'n kenmerkende swart streep op die rug, swart bene en swart ringe om die stert. Hulle merk hul roetes met uitskeidings van die per-ineaalkliere. Die afskeiding is in die verlede in parfuumvervaardiging gebruik. Hulle vreet insekte, reptiele, klein soogdiere en veldvrugte. Twee tot vier kleintjies word na 'n draagtyd van nege weke gebore.

LA CIVETTE

Son pelage est gris taché de noir avec une ligne de poils noirs caractéristique sur l'échine. Ses pattes sont noires et sa queue est striée de noir et blanc. Elle délim-ite son territoire à l'aide de sécrétions des glandes anales. On utilisait autrefois cette matière odorante dans la fabrication des parfums. C'est un animal nocturne qui se nourrit d'insectes, de reptiles, de petits mammifères et de fruits sauvages. La civette met bas de deux à quatre petits. Elle peut vivre pendant 45 ans.

ZIBETKATZEN

Zibetkatzen haben ein graues, schwarzgeflecktes Fell mit einem Kamm von dunklen Haaren auf dem Rücken. Die Beine sind schwarz, und der Schwanz ist schwarzweiß gestreift. Sie markieren ihre Routen mit einem Sekret, das früher für die Parfümherstellung benutzt wurde. Sie sind Nachttiere und leben von Insekten, Reptilien, kleinen Säugetieren und Wildfrüchten. Nach einer Tragzeit von neun Wochen werfen sie zwei bis vier Jungen.

Civettictis civetta

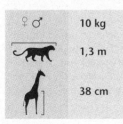

♀ ♂   10 kg

1,3 m

38 cm

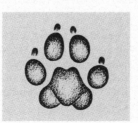

KRUGER

71

Felis serval

SERVAL

This long-legged cat has a small head, a short tail, large ears and attractive spots and stripes on the back. Mainly nocturnal and solitary, it is sometimes active in the early morning and late afternoon, and may be seen in pairs or small family groups. It feeds on rodents, birds, snakes, lizards and locusts. After a 70-day gestation period, one to three young are born, usually during the warmer months.

TIERBOSKAT

Die tierboskat het 'n klein koppie, groot ore, 'n kort stert, aantreklike kolle en strepe op die rug, en lang bene. Hulle is hoofsaaklik naglewend en alleenlopers, maar kom ook in pare en familiegroepe voor. Hulle vreet knaagdiere, akkedisse, voëls, slange en sprinkane. Een tot drie kleintjies per werpsel word gewoonlik in die warmer maande gebore, na 'n draagtyd van 70 dae.

LE SERVAL

C'est un félin aux longues pattes, à la tête petite, à la queue courte et aux grandes oreilles. Il a aussi d'élégantes taches et rayures sur l'échine. Essentiellement nocturne et solitaire, le serval se nourrit normalement de rongeurs, d'oiseaux, de serpents, de lézards et de sauterelles. Les animaux n'habitent presque jamais loin des points d'eau. Après une période de gestation de 70 jours, la femelle met bas d'un à trois petits, généralement à la saison chaude.

SERVALKATZE

Diese langbeinige Katze hat einen kleinen Kopf, kurzen Schwanz, große Ohren und ein hübsch markiertes Fell mit Flecken und Streifen auf dem Rücken. Sie ist ein Einzelgänger sowie ein Nachttier und ernährt sich von Nagetieren, Vögeln, Schlangen, Eidechsen und Heuschrecken. Sie lebt im hohen Gras und meist in Wassernähe. Nach einer Tragzeit von 70 Tagen und meistens in den wärmeren Monaten wirft sie ein bis drei Junge.

Felis serval

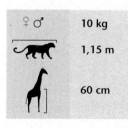

♀ ♂   **10 kg**

   1,15 m

   60 cm

KRUGER,
MARAKELE,
ADDO ELEPHANT,
TSITSIKAMMA

73

Felis caracal

CARACAL

Also known as the Lynx, the Caracal is stockier than the Serval and its fur varies in colour from light red to brick red. The ears have distinct tufts at the ends. Caracals are nocturnal but are sometimes seen on cool days. They feed mainly on birds, mammals and reptiles but may also capture medium-sized antelope such as Duiker and Steenbok. Litters consist of two or three young.

ROOIKAT

Rooikatte is frisser as tierboskatte. Die pels is ligrooi tot baksteenrooi. Die ore het duidelike haarklossies op die punte. Rooikatte is alleenlopend, hoofsaaklik nagdiere, maar word op koel dae gesien. Hulle vreet veral voëls, soogdiere en reptiele, maar vang ook mediumgrootte wildsbokke soos duikers en steenbokke. Twee of drie kleintjies word na 'n draagtyd van drie maande gebore.

LE CARACAL

Appelé aussi lynx, le caracal est d'apparence plus robuste que le serval et son pelage est d'une couleur rousse assez vive variant en intensité. Ses oreilles pointues sont garnies d'un pinceau de poils. C'est un félin nocturne, bien qu'on puisse l'apercevoir lorsqu'il fait frais. Il se nourrit surtout d'oiseaux, de mammifères et de reptiles mais aussi de petites antilopes tels que les céphalophes et les steenboks. Le caracal a une portée de deux ou trois petits.

KARAKAL

Der Wüstenluchs, wie das Tier auch genannt wird, ist stämmiger als die Servalkatze. Sein Fell variiert von hellrot bis dunkelrot. Er ist unverkennbar mit seinen in Haarpinseln endenden Ohren. Obwohl diese Füchse nachts aktiv sind, kann man sie an kühlen Tagen auch tagsüber sehen. Sie ernähren sich von Vögeln, Säuge- und Kriechtieren, gelegentlich erbeuten sie auch Antilopen. Normalerweise sind sie Einzelgänger. Ihr Wurf umfaßt zwei bis drei Junge.

Felis caracal

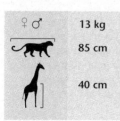

13 kg

85 cm

40 cm

All Parks
Alle parke
Toutes les Reserves
Alle Reservate

Acinonyx jubatus

CHEETAH

The markings of the Cheetah differ from those of the Leopard in being 'solid' rather than appearing as rosettes. This is the only cat that cannot fully retract its claws. Cheetahs prefer open savanna, relying on speed to capture prey; they can top 100 km/h over short distances. Two to four cubs are born after a three-month gestation period. Life expectancy is 15 years.

JAGLUIPERD

Die jagluiperd verskil van die luiperd op grond daarvan dat sy kolle solied is. Die kop het 'n duidelike 'traanstreep' vanaf die oog na die mondhoeke. Die liggaam is slank en gebou om vinnig te kan beweeg. Die toonnaels kan nie terugtrek nie. Hulle verkies oop savanna omdat hulle spoed nodig het om hul prooi te vang. Twee tot vier kleintjies word gebore na 'n draagtyd van drie maande.

LE GUEPARD

Le guépard se distingue du léopard par ses taches qui ressortent clairement, sa face marquée de deux lignes noires caractéristiques allant des yeux jusqu'aux coins de la gueule. Ses griffes ne sont pas rétractiles comme celles des autres félins. Habitant des savanes, le guépard compte sur sa vitesse pour capturer ses proies. Il est capable d'atteindre une vitesse de 100 km à l'heure. Après une période de gestation de trois mois, la femelle met bas de deux à quatre petits.

GEPARD

Seine deutliche Fellmarkierung und die dunklen 'Tränenspuren', die vom Auge bis zum Maul verlaufen, sind typisch für das Tier. Der Gepard ist die einzige Wildkatze, die ihre Krallen nicht einziehen kann. Er liebt offenes Gras-land und verläßt sich auf seine Geschwindigkeit, um seine Beute zu fangen; über kurze Entfernungen erreicht der Gepard eine Geschwindigkeit von 100 km/h. Seine Lebenserwartung liegt bei 15 Jahren.

Acinonyx jubatus

♀ ♂ 50 kg

100 km/h

75 cm

Kruger,
Kalahari Gemsbok

Panthera pardus

LEOPARD

A solitary, nocturnal predator, the Leopard prefers densely wooded river banks and mountainous areas. It differs from the Cheetah in having its spots arranged in rosettes. The body is short and stocky. Leopards feed on a variety of animals, often hiding their prey in trees. Two or three cubs are born after a three-month gestation period. Life expectancy is 20 years.

LUIPERD

'n Alleenlopende, nagtelike roofdier. Verkies rivieroewers of bergagtige streke met digte bos. Die kolle is rosetvormig; die liggaam is korter en stewiger as die jagluiperd s'n en die naels kan teruggetrek word. Luiperds vreet 'n verskeidenheid prooi, en sal dikwels hul prooi in 'n boom bêre. Twee of drie kleintjies word gebore na 'n draagtyd van drie maande.

LE LEOPARD

Le léopard est un prédateur solitaire et nocturne qui fréquente les berges boisées des rivières et aussi les endroits montagneux. Il se distingue du guépard par le dessin de ses taches. Le corps de cet animal est petit et ramassé. Le léopard se nourrit de proies variées qu'il cache souvent dans les arbres. Après une période de gestation de trois mois, la femelle met bas deux ou trois petits. Le léopard peut vivre pendant 20 ans.

LEOPARD

Dieser zur Nachtzeit aktive Einzelgänger bevorzugt als Habitat dicht bewachsene Flußufer und bergige Gegenden. Seine rosettenartigen Fellflecken unterscheiden ihn vom Gepard. Der Körper ist kurz und stämmig. Dieses Raubtier macht Jagd auf viele Tiere und versteckt seine Beute oft in Bäumen. Zwei oder drei Junge werden nach einer dreimonatigen Tragzeit geboren. Die Lebenserwartung eines Leoparden liegt bei 20 Jahren.

Panthera pardus

♀♂ 60 kg

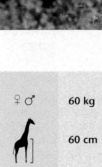 60 cm

KRUGER,
MARAKELE,
AUGRABIES FALLS,
KALAHARI GEMSBOK,
RICHTERSVELD,
TSITSIKAMMA

Panthera leo

LION

Lions are social predators, living in groups of up to 30 individuals. They are noted to have killed animals as large as Elephant and Hippo. Mating takes place throughout the year, and one to four cubs are born after a gestation period of about three months. The Tshokwane population of the Kruger National Park sometimes produces white offspring due to genetic deviation.

LEEU

Leeus is sosiale roofdiere, en kom voor in groepe van tot 30 diere. Leeus het al diere soos olifante en seekoeie gevang. Hulle paar dwarsdeur die jaar, met 'n hoogtepunt in die herfs of vroeë winter. Een tot vier welpies word gebore na 'n draagtyd van drie maande. Die Tshokwane-leeubevolking van die Krugerwild-tuin lewer soms wit leeus op, as gevolg van genetiese afwykings.

LE LION

Le lion est un animal sociable. Ce prédateur vit en groupes qui peuvent compter près de 30 bêtes. On sait qu'il est capable de tuer des éléphants et des hippopo-tames. Il s'accouple toute l'année mais en particulier en automne ou au début de l'hiver. Après une gestation de trois mois environ, la lionne met bas d'un à quatre lionceaux. Le lion peut vivre pendant 20 ans. On aperçoit parfois dans le Parc Kruger des lionceaux blancs, particularité due à un phénomène génétique.

LÖWE

Der Löwe ist als geselliges Raubtier bekannt; sie leben in Rudeln bis zu 30 Tieren. Löwen sind sogar fähig, Elefanten und Nilpferde zu töten. Sie paaren sich das ganze Jahr hindurch. Sie werfen ein bis vier Junge nach einer Tragzeit von etwa drei Monaten. Ihre Lebenserwartung liegt bei 20 Jahren. Die Jungen bleiben zwei Jahre bei der Mutter, ehe sie eigene Wege gehen. Die Tshokwane-Löwen gebären gelegentlich aufgrund genetischer Abweichungen Albinos.

Panthera leo

♀ ♂ **200 kg**

60 km/h

1,25 m

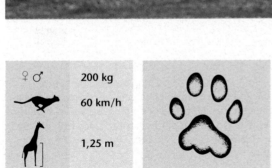

Kruger,
Kalahari Gemsbok

Loxodonta africana

ELEPHANT

Elephants are the largest land mammals in the world. They are hunted for their ivory and endangered in some parts of Africa. However, in many South African national parks their high numbers result in considerable damage to vegetation, and for this reason population-control programmes are often essential. One calf is born after a gestation period of 22 months. Life expectancy is 60 years.

OLIFANT

Olifante is die grootste landsoogdiere ter wêreld. Hulle word vir hul ivoor gejag, en is bedreig in baie dele van Afrika. In die Suid-Afrikaanse nasionale parke neem hul getalle egter toe, wat lei tot groot skade aan plantegroei, en bevolkingsbeheer dus noodsaak. Troppe bestaan uit koeie en kalwers; bulle is alleenlopend of vorm los troppe. Een kalf word gebore na 'n draagtyd van 22 maande.

L'ELEPHANT

C'est le plus grand mammifère terrestre du monde. Chassé pour son ivoire, c'est une espèce en danger dans certaines parties d'Afrique. Toutefois, dans les parcs nationaux d'Afrique du Sud, les éléphants sont très nombreux. Un troupeau d'éléphants est composé de femelles et des petits; les mâles sont solitaires ou forment des troupeaux de mâles. Après 15 mois de gestation, la femelle met bas un seul petit. L'éléphant peut vivre pendant 60 ans.

ELEFANT

Der Elefant ist das größte Säugetier der Welt. Sein Elfenbein ist eine begehrte Beute, und in einigen Teilen Afrikas ist sein Überleben gefährdet. Herden bestehen aus Kühen und Kälbern; Bullen sind Einzelgänger oder gruppieren sich in Junggesellenherden. Bullen schließen sich nur zur Begattung einer Kuh an. Ein Kalb wird nach einer Tragzeit von 22 Monaten geboren. Die Lebenserwartung der Dickhäuter liegt bei 60 Jahren.

Loxodonta africana

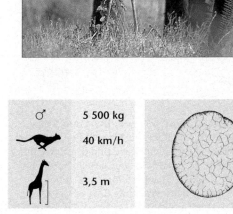

♂ 5 500 kg

40 km/h

3,5 m

KRUGER,
MARAKELE,
ADDO ELEPHANT

Diceros bicornis

HOOK-LIPPED RHINOCEROS

This rhino, also known as the Black Rhinoceros, is characterized by its elongated, slightly pointed upper lip which overlaps the lower. These browsers use their upper lip and horn to hook branches within reach. They are less social than the Square-lipped Rhinoceros.When endangered, the cow runs ahead of the calf. A single calf is born after a 15-month gestation period.

SWARTRENOSTER

Die swartrenoster het 'n verlengde, effens gepunte bolip wat oor die onderlip strek. Hulle is donkergrys van kleur. Swartrenosters is blaarvreters wat die bolip en die horing gebruik om takke te haak en nader te trek. Hulle is meer alleenlopend as die witrenoster. Wanneer bedreig, sal die koei voor die kalf hardloop. 'n Enkele kalfie word gebore na 'n draagtyd van 15 maande.

LE RHINOCEROS NOIR

On le reconnaît à sa lèvre supérieure, allongée et légèrement pointue, qui chevauche sa lèvre inférieure. Il se nourrit de feuilles et utilise sa lèvre supérieure et sa corne pour attraper les branchages. C'est un animal moins sociable que le rhinocéros blanc. La femelle ne met bas qu'un seul petit après une période de gestation de 15 mois. En cas de danger, la femelle court devant le petit. Cette espèce peut vivre pendant 45 ans.

SPITZMAULNASHORN

Dieses Nashorn ist auch als das Schwarze Nashorn bekannt. Es ist durch eine verlängerte, etwas hakenförmige Oberlippe, die über der Unterlippe hinaushängt, gekennzeichnet. Als Äser benutzen sie die Oberlippe und das Horn, um Zweige festzuhaken, die sie dann fressen. Sie sind nicht sehr gesellig und können auch recht gefährlich werden. Ein Kalb wird nach 15 Monaten geboren. Bei Gefahr läuft die Kuh vor das Kalb. Die Lebenserwartung liegt bei 45 Jahren.

Diceros bicornis

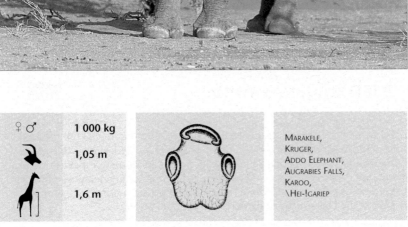

♀♂ 1 000 kg

1,05 m

1,6 m

MARAKELE,
KRUGER,
ADDO ELEPHANT,
AUGRABIES FALLS,
KAROO,
\HEI-!GARIEP

Ceratotherium simum

SQUARE-LIPPED RHINOCEROS

Also known as the White Rhinoceros, this species is characterized by a broad, flat lower lip and a distinctive hump on the neck. They are grazers. They are fond of mud baths which help to control body temperature and parasites. Bulls are very territorial and create distinct dung middens. When endangered, the calf runs ahead of its mother. The gestation period is 16 months, and usually a single calf is born.

WITRENOSTER

Die witrenoster word gekenmerk deur 'n breë, plat onderlip en 'n kenmerkende skof. Hulle is grasvreters. Witrenosterbulle is baie territoriaal, en bou duidelike territoriale mishope. Hulle bad graag in modder om hul liggaamstemperatuur te beheer en parasiete in toom te hou. Wanneer bedreig, hardloop die kalf voor die ma. 'n Enkele kleintjie word gebore na 'n draagtyd van 16 maande.

LE RHINOCEROS BLANC

On le reconnaît à sa lèvre supérieure large et carrée ainsi qu'à la bosse de son échine. C'est un herbivore qui aime tout particulièrement les bains de boue qui lui permettent de régler la température de son corps et de le débarasser des parasites. Les mâles sont très territoriaux et marquent leur territoire à l'aide de déjections. En cas d'alerte, le petit court devant sa mère. La femelle ne met bas qu'un seul petit après 16 mois. Cette espèce peut vivre pendant 45 ans.

BREITMAULNASHORN

Es ist auch als das Weiße Nashorn bekannt, und wird durch eine breite, flache Unterlippe gekennzeichnet sowie einem ausgeprägten Höcker am Hals. Nashörner sind Äser und lieben Schlammbäder, die ihre Körpertemperatur regulieren und Parasiten verjagen. Die Bullen grenzen ihren Bereich durch ihre Exkremente ab und verteidigen es auch. Ein Junges kommt nach 16 Monaten zur Welt. Die Lebenserwartung der Tiere liegt bei 45 Jahren.

Ceratotherium simum

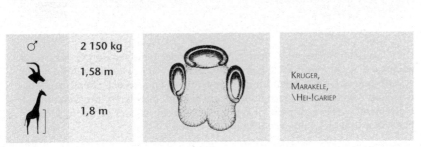

♂	2 150 kg
	1,58 m
	1,8 m

KRUGER,
MARAKELE,
\HEI-!GARIEP

87

Hippopotamus amphibius

HIPPOPOTAMUS

These ungulates inhabit rivers or dams and leave the water at night to graze. Hippos feed exclusively on grass and establish pear-shaped territories fanning out from their pools. During their nocturnal excursions they form wide footpaths. After an eight-month gestation period one young is born in secluded reedbeds close to water. Life expectancy is 54 years.

SEEKOEI

'n Rivierbewoner wat bedags naby water bly, en snags die water verlaat om te wei. Hulle word ook in damme gevind. Seekoeie is grasvreters. Op hulle nagtelike togte trap hulle breë voetpaaie oop. Hulle merk hul gebiede deur die mis met die stert stukkend te slaan en te sprei. Een kleintjie word in afgesonderde rietbeddings naby water gebore na 'n draagtyd van agt maande.

L'HIPPOPOTAME

Ongulé herbivore, il vit dans les rivières qu'il quitte, à la nuit tombante, pour brouter les herbes des berges. A la sortie des mares, il marque son territoire qui se déploie sous forme d'éventail. Lors de sa sortie nocturne, il ouvre des sentiers et marque alors son territoire en étalant ses déjections avec de rapides coups de queue. Après huit mois de gestation, la femelle met bas son petit dans les roseaux à proximité de l'eau. L'hippopotame peut vivre pendant 54 ans.

NILPFERD

Diese Land- und Wassertiere leben in Flüssen oder Dämmen und verlassen nur nachts das Wasser zum Äsen. Nilpferde leben von Gras. Um ihren Pfuhl herum schaffen sie sich ein birnenförmiges Refugium. Wenn sie sich abends auf Wanderschaft begeben, treten sie breite Pfade aus und markieren ihre Gebiete mit Exkrementen. Junge werden zu Land, aber nahe am Wasser geboren. Die Lebenserwartung der Nilpferde liegt bei 54 Jahren.

Hippopotamus amphibius

♀ ♂   1 500 kg

1,5 m

KRUGER,
ZUURBERG,
MARAKELE

AARDVARK

A solitary animal, active mainly at night, the Aardvark feeds on termites and ants. It is well known for its ability to dig holes and tunnels with its strong claws. The abandoned shelters of Aardvarks are often used by animals such as Hyaenas, Porcupines, Warthogs and Jackals. After a seven-month gestation period a single young is born. Life expectancy is ten years.

ERDVARK

'n Alleenlopende dier wat hoofsaaklik snags aktief is. Hulle leef van termiete en miere, en is bekend vir hul vermoë om gate en tonnels met hulle sterk kloue te grawe. Hulle grawe tydelike en permanente skuilings, wat dikwels deur ander diere soos hiëna's, ystervarke, vlakvarke en jakkalse gebruik word. 'n Enkele kleintjie word gebore na 'n draagtyd van sewe maande.

L'ORYCTEROPE

Animal solitaire et nocturne, il se nourrit de termites et de fourmis. Il préfère les régions broussailleuses. Excellent terrassier, il creuse des trous et des tunnels avec ses griffes acérées. Lorsqu'il abandonne son gîte, d'autres animaux tels que la hyène, le porc-épic, le phacochère et le chacal l'habitent à leur tour. Après une période de gestation de sept mois, la femelle met bas un seul petit. L'oryc-térope peut vivre pendant dix ans.

AMEISENBÄR

Der Ameisenbär, auch Erdferkel genannt, ist ein Einzelgänger und meist ein Nachttier. Er sieht schlecht, hört dafür aber ausgezeichnet. Er lebt von Termi-ten und Ameisen und gräbt mit seinen Klauen Höhlen und Tunnel. Verläßt er seinen Bau, übernehmen ihn oft andere Tiere wie Hyänen, Wildschweine und Schakale. Ein Junges wird nach siebenmonatiger Tragzeit geboren. Die Lebens-erwartung dieser Tiere liegt bei zehn Jahren.

Orycteropus afer

♀ ♂	55 kg
	1,7 m

Kruger, Marakele,
Addo Elephant,
Mountain Zebra,
Kalahari Gemsbok,
Zuurberg, Karoo, Tankwa
Karoo, \Hei-!Gariep,
Augrabies Falls, West Coast

91

Phacochoerus aethiopicus

WARTHOG

These greyish, sparsely haired animals have wart-like growths on the head: males have two pairs and females one pair. They feed on grass and are active by day, sheltering in holes at night. The tail is held upright when running, to maintain contact in tall grass. The upper tusks are used for defence. Two or three young are born after a gestation period of 170 days. Life expectancy is 20 years.

VLAKVARK

Die vratagtige uitgroeisels aan die kop is kenmerkend – twee paar by die beer en een paar by die sog. Hulle is grasvreters en bedags aktief, terwyl hulle snags in gate skuil. Hulle lig die stert regop as hulle hardloop, om kontak te behou in lang gras. Die boonste slagtande word effektief vir verdediging gebruik. Twee of drie kleintjies word gebore na 'n draagtyd van 170 dae.

LE PHACOCHERE

Cet animal de couleur grisâtre et à la peau presque nue se distingue par des excroissances sur la tête, semblables à des verrues; deux paires de verrues caractérisent le mâle tandis que la femelle n'en a qu'une. Il est actif pendant le jour et se nourrit d'herbes. Lorsqu'il court dans les hautes herbes, il dresse sa queue à la verticale pour garder le contact avec le reste de la bande. Après 170 jours, la femelle met bas deux ou trois petits. L'animal peut vivre pendant 20 ans.

WARZENSCHWEIN

Diese spärlich behaarten, graufarbenen Tiere werden durch warzenähnliche Auswüchse auf dem Kopf gekennzeichnet, von denen das Männchen zwei, das weibliche Tier eins hat. Sie fressen Gras; nachts suchen sie Schutz in Höhlen. Wenn sie laufen, zeigt ihr Schwanz nach oben – ein Kontaktsymbol – ebenso bei Angriff oder Flucht. Zwei oder drei Junge werden nach einer Tragzeit von 170 Tagen geboren. Ihre Lebenserwartung liegt bei 20 Jahren.

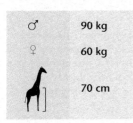

♂	90 kg
♀	60 kg
	70 cm

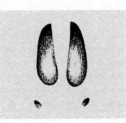

KRUGER,
MARAKELE,
\HEI-!GARIEP,
GOLDEN GATE
HIGHLANDS

Potamochoerus porcus

BUSHPIG

Nocturnal animals with a characteristic snout, Bushpigs are gregarious, occurring in groups of up to 12. They feed on grass, grass rhizomes, bulbs, wild fruit, earthworms and insect larvae. The sows construct secluded nests of grass. Dominant boars will aggressively drive off other boars. Three to eight young are born. Life expectancy is 20 years.

BOSVARK

'n Nagdier met 'n kenmerkende snoet. Hulle is sosiaal, en leef in groepe van tot 12 diere. Hulle vreet graag gras, graswortels, erdwurms, inseklarwes, bolle en veldvrugte. Die sog bou 'n nes van gras in afgesonderde gebiede. Die beer is dominant en sal ander bere aggressief verdryf. Die gevaarlike, onderste slagtande word vir selfverdediging gebruik. Drie tot agt kleintjies word gebore.

LE POTAMOCHERE

Le potamochère est un animal nocturne que caractérise son groin. Il est grégaire et vit en petites hardes de 12 individus au maximum. L'animal se nourrit d'herbes, de racines, de bulbes, de vers de terre, de larves d'insectes et de fruits sauvages. Il habite les régions broussailleuses et les forêts. Les mâles dominants et agressifs évincent les autres mâles. La femelle met bas de trois à huit petits. Le potamochère peut vivre pendant 20 ans.

BUSCHSCHWEIN

Das Tier ist zur Nachtzeit unterwegs und besitzt ein sehr charakteristisches Grunzen. Buschschweine sind gesellig und rotten sich bis zu 12 Tieren zusammen. Sie leben von Gras, Grasrhizomen, Knollen, Erdwürmern, Insektenlarven und Wildfrüchten. Die Sau baut abgelegene Grasnester. Eindringlinge werden durch den herrschenden Keiler aggressiv vertrieben. Eine Sau hat drei bis acht Junge. Die Lebenserwartung liegt bei 20 Jahren.

Potamochoerus porcus

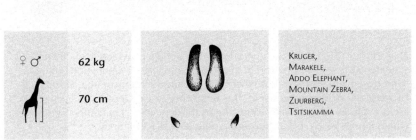

♀ ♂   62 kg

🦒 | 70 cm

KRUGER,
MARAKELE,
ADDO ELEPHANT,
MOUNTAIN ZEBRA,
ZUURBERG,
TSITSIKAMMA

Equus zebra zebra

CAPE MOUNTAIN ZEBRA

Cape Mountain Zebras are diurnal and occur in more mountainous regions. They can be distinguished from Burchell's Zebra by the distinct dewlap, 'grid-iron' pattern on the rump above the tail and in lacking 'shadow' stripes. The belly is white and stripes encircle the legs. These Zebras are predominantly grazers, but will occasionally browse. A single foal is born after a 12-month gestation period.

BERGKWAGGA

Die bergkwagga kom in meer bergagtige gebiede voor. Daar is 'n duidelike keelvel aanwesig en 'n ruitpatroon op die kruis bokant die stert. Daar is geen skadustrepe nie, en die pens is wit. Strepe strek om die bene. Bergkwaggas is daglewende grasvreters met 'n sterk sosiale struktuur. Hingste veg dikwels om dominansie. Een vul word gewoonlik gebore na 'n draagtyd van 12 maande.

LE ZEBRE DE MONTAGNE

C'est un animal diurne qui vit dans les régions montagneuses. Il se distingue du zèbre de Burchell par son fanon et par le motif en 'grille' de sa croupe au-dessus de la queue ainsi que par l'absence de bandes ombrées entre les rayures noires. Son ventre est blanc et ses pattes entourées de rayures. Il se nourrit surtout d'herbes et à l'occasion de feuilles. La femelle met bas un seul petit après une gestation de 12 mois. Le zèbre de montagne peut vivre pendant 35 ans.

KAPBERGZEBRA

Man trifft die Tiere am Tage überwiegend in bergigen Gebieten an. Sie unterscheiden sich vom Steppenzebra durch eine auffällige Wamme und einem 'Gittereisen' auf ihrem Hinterteil sowie fehlende Schattenstreifen. Der Bauch ist weiß, die Beine sind gestreift. Das Bergzebra ist ein Grasfresser, gelegentlich äst es auch. Es sind gesellige Tiere, die in Herden leben. Ein Fohlen wird nach einem Jahr geboren. Die Lebenserwartung liegt bei 35 Jahren.

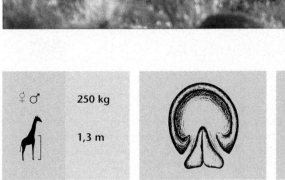

♀ ♂   **250 kg**

1,3 m

MOUNTAIN ZEBRA,
BONTEBOK,
ZUURBERG,
KAROO

Equus burchellii

BURCHELL'S ZEBRA

Burchell's Zebra differs from the Cape Mountain Zebra by having stripes which encircle the belly, brown 'shadow' stripes and no dewlap. These plains animals prefer short-grass areas. They occur in family groups and are nomadic, often forming huge herds during seasonal migrations. After a 12-month gestation period a single foal is born. Life expectancy is 35 years.

BONTKWAGGA

Die strepe strek om die pens en vertoon bruin skadustrepe. Daar is geen keelvel of ruitpatroon nie. Bontkwaggas is vlaktediere wat in familiegroepe woon. Hulle is nomadies en vorm dikwels groot groepe tydens seisoenale trekke. Hulle verkies kortgrasgebiede, en migreer dikwels van somer- na winterweiding. 'n Enkele vul word gebore na 'n draagtyd van 12 maande.

LE ZEBRE DE BURCHELL

Contrairement au zèbre de montagne, cette espèce possède des rayures tout autour du ventre ainsi que des bandes ombrées entre les rayures noires, et il n'a pas de fanon. C'est un habitant des plaines qui préfère les herbes courtes. Il vit en petits groupes et mène une existence nomade. A la saison des migrations, les zèbres se rassemblent pour former d'immenses troupeaux. La femelle met bas un petit après une gestation de 12 mois. Le zèbre peut vivre pendant 25 ans.

BURCHELLS STEPPENZEBRA

Es unterscheidet sich vom Bergzebra durch seine Bauchstreifen und braunen Schattenstreifen sowie der fehlenden Wamme. Diese Tiere bevorzugen offene Savannen. Die Steppenzebras kommen in Gruppen vor und sind Nomaden. Oft wachsen sie während ihrer Wanderung von Sommer- zu Winterweiden zu Riesenherden an. Ein Fohlen wird nach zwölfmonatiger Tragzeit geboren. Die Lebenserwartung der Tiere liegt bei 35 Jahren.

Equus burchellii

♀ ♂   300 kg

1,3 m

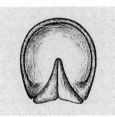

KRUGER,
MARAKELE,
GOLDEN GATE HIGHLANDS,
\HEI-!GARIEP

Giraffa camelopardalis

GIRAFFE

Giraffes prefer open woodland with a dominance of thorn trees. They are most vulnerable when drinking water and thus very alert at these times. They occur in groups which may number up to 30; bulls associate with cows only temporarily. Bulls often fight by sparring, hitting one another with the horns. After a 15-month gestation period a single calf is born. Life expectancy is 28 years.

KAMEELPERD

Die kameelperd verkies oop bosveld met heelwat doringbome. Hulle is daglewend, en kom in klein groepe voor. Bulle veg dikwels deur mekaar met die kop te slaan. Gevolglik is hul horings kaal bo en baie dikker. Kameelperde is baie kwesbaar wanneer hulle water drink en is dan baie waaksaam. 'n Enkele kalf word in 'n staande posisie gebore na 'n draagtyd van 15 maande.

LA GIRAFE

La girafe habite la savane émaillée d'arbustes et d'épineux. Particulièrement vulnérable lorsqu'elle s'abreuve, elle se tient aux aguets lorsqu'elle se désaltère. C'est un animal actif le jour et la nuit. Elle vit en groupes d'une trentaine d'individus. Lors de bagarres, les mâles usent de leurs cornes dont l'extrémité est sans poils. La femelle met bas un seul petit après une gestation de 15 mois. La girafe peut vivre pendant 28 ans.

GIRAFFE

Giraffen bevorzugen buschiges, mit Dornengestrüpp bewachsenes Gelände. Besonders gefährdet und daher sehr wachsam sind sie beim Trinken. Durch ihre Länge erreichen sie Nahrung außerhalb der Reichweite anderer Tiere. Sie sind am Tag und in der Nacht aktiv. Bis zu 30 Tiere leben zusammen. Die Bullen führen Scheinkämpfe aus, indem sie mit ihren Hörner aufeinanderprallen. Nach 15 Monaten wird ein Kalb geboren. Die Lebenserwartung liegt bei 28 Jahren.

Giraffa camelopardalis

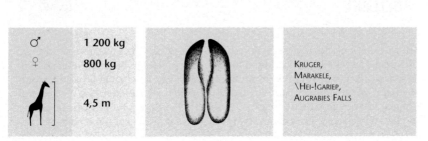

♂	1 200 kg
♀	800 kg
	4,5 m

KRUGER,
MARAKELE,
\HEI-!GARIEP,
AUGRABIES FALLS

Syncerus caffer

BUFFALO

These animals are predominantly grazers. Their preferred habitat of dense, tall grass has diminished in recent years. Both sexes have horns, those of the bulls being more massive. They occur in large herds that move seasonally. Old bulls may be solitary but bachelor herds also occur. A single calf is born after a gestation period of 11 months. Life expectancy is 25 years.

BUFFEL

Die buffel se habitat het erg ingekrimp. Hulle is hoofsaaklik grasvreters, en benodig volop lang gras en oppervlakwater. Beide geslagte het horings; die bul s'n is baie groter. Hulle kom voor in groot troppe wat seisoenaal beweeg. Ou bulle word dikwels alleenlopend, maar bultroppe word ook gevorm. 'n Enkele kalf word gebore na 'n draagtyd van 11 maande.

LE BUFFLE

Cet animal herbivore vit dans la savane. Il affectionne les bains de boue et se tient près des points d'eau. Mâle et femelle ont tous les deux des cornes, bien que celles du mâle soient plus massives. Les buffles vivent en vastes troupeaux qui se déplacent au gré des migrations. Les vieux mâles sont généralement solitaires mais il arrive qu'ils forment de petits groupes. La femelle met bas un seul petit après une gestation de 11 mois. Le buffle peut vivre pendant 25 ans.

BÜFFEL

Diese Tiere benötigen dichtes, hohes Gras und Wasser. Es gibt nur noch wenig adäquate Habitate in Afrika. Büffel lieben Schlammbäder. Beide Geschlechter besitzen Hörner; die des Bullen sind aber massiver. Sie leben in großen Herden, die jahreszeitlich bedingt auf Wanderschaft gehen. Alte Bullen sind oft Einzelgänger, aber es gibt auch Junggesellenherden. Ein Kalb wird pro Jahr und pro Weibchen geboren. Die Lebenserwartung eines Büffels liegt bei 25 Jahren.

Syncerus caffer

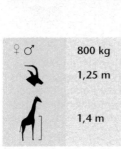

♀ ♂	**800 kg**
	1,25 m
	1,4 m

KRUGER,
MARAKELE,
ADDO ELEPHANT,
\HEI-!GARIEP

Connochaetes gnou

BLACK WILDEBEEST

Black Wildebeest are gregarious, favour open grassveld and are dependent on water. They are mainly grazers. Black Wildebeest bulls are known for their stiff-legged cantering, advertising their territorial ownership during the rut when other males join bachelor herds. After an eight-and-a-half-month gestation period a single calf is born during summer. Life expectancy is 20 years.

SWARTWILDEBEES

Hierdie grasvreters is tropdiere wat oop grasveld verkies, en afhanklik is van water. Bulle is territoriaal tydens paartyd, en ander bulle sluit dan by vrygesel-troppe aan. Swartwildebeeste is bekend vir hul stywebeen galop, waarmee hulle hul territoriums markeer. Hulle is hoofsaaklik grasvreters. 'n Enkele kalf word in die somer gebore na 'n draagtyd van agt en 'n half maand.

LE GNOU NOIR

C'est un animal grégaire qui habite les vastes étendues herbeuses et qui a besoin d'être à proximité des points d'eau. Il se nourrit principalement d'herbes. A la saison du rut, le mâle dominant marque son territoire d'un galop raide carac-téristique. Le gnou est connu par son comportement excentrique. La femelle ne met bas qu'un seul petit après une période de gestation de huit mois et demi. Le gnou noir peut vivre pendant 20 ans.

WEIßSCHWANZGNU

Diese geselligen, meist grasfressenden Tiere bevorzugen das offene Grasland, und sie sind vom Wasser abhängig. Die Bullen sind für ihren steifbeinigen Tanz während der Brunftzeit bekannt. Sie markieren mit dem Tanz ihren individuel-len Brunftplatz. Jeweils ein Kalb wird nach einer Tragzeit von ungefähr achtein-halb Monaten im Sommer geboren. Die Lebenserwartung der Weißschwanzgnus liegt bei 20 Jahren.

Connochaetes gnou

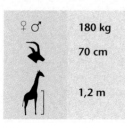

♀ ♂   **180 kg**

70 cm

1,2 m

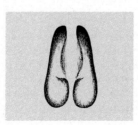

MOUNTAIN ZEBRA,
GOLDEN GATE HIGHLANDS,
\HEI-!GARIEP

Connochaetes taurinus

BLUE WILDEBEEST

These gregarious animals are well known for their annual migrations when they congregate in huge herds. They prefer open woodland with water. They are grazers with a preference for short grass. Bulls display territorial behaviour during the rut, when other bulls join bachelor herds. A single calf is born after a gestation period of eight and a half months. Life expectancy is 20 years.

BLOUWILDEBEES

Hierdie kuddediere is bekend vir hul jaarlikse migrasie, waartydens hulle in groot troppe versamel. Hulle verkies oop boomsavanna met water. Bulle vertoon slegs territoriale gedrag tydens paartyd; ondergeskikte bulle vorm dan vrygeseltroppe. Blouwildebeeste is grasvreters met 'n voorkeur vir kort gras. 'n Enkele kalf word gebore na 'n draagtyd van agt en 'n half maand.

LE GNOU BLEU

Bien connus pour leurs migrations annuelles, les gnous bleus sont grégaires et se rassemblent en d'immenses troupeaux. Ils vivent dans les régions boisées à proximité de points d'eau. Herbivores, ils préfèrent les herbes courtes. A la saison du rut, les mâles dominants marquent leur territoire. Entre novembre et décembre, la femelle met bas un seul petit après une gestation de huit mois et demi. Le gnou bleu peut vivre pendant 20 ans.

STREIFENGNU

Diese geselligen Tiere sind für ihre alljährlichen Wanderungen, für die sie sich zu Riesenherden zusammenfinden, wohlbekannt. Sie bevorzugen Buschsavannen mit Wasser. Die Tiere lieben besonders kurzes Gras. Während der Brunftzeit grenzen die Bullen ihr Terrain voneinander ab. Zwischen November und Dezember wird nach circa acht Monaten ein Kalb geboren. Die Lebenserwartung der Tiere liegt bei 20 Jahren.

Connochaetes taurinus

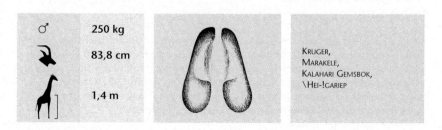

♂ 250 kg

83,8 cm

1,4 m

KRUGER,
MARAKELE,
KALAHARI GEMSBOK,
\HEI-!GARIEP

107

Taurotragus oryx

ELAND

Eland are the largest antelope in Africa. They inhabit desert scrub to montane regions as well as bushveld. They are mainly browsers but will graze freshly sprouting grass. Eland occur in small herds, but will congregate in large herds when nomadic. They are excellent jumpers. A single calf is born after a nine-month gestation period. Life expectancy is 12 years.

ELAND

Die eland is die grootste antiloop in Afrika. Hulle kom voor in woestynhabitatte, bergagtige dele en bosveld, en is nie afhanklik van oppervlakwater nie. Elande kom in klein troppe voor. Wanneer nomadies, trek hulle saam in groot troppe. Hulle kan baie hoog spring. Elande is hoofsaaklik blaarvreters, maar sal ook nuwe gras bewei. 'n Enkele kalf word gebore na 'n draagtyd van nege maande.

L'ELAND

C'est la plus grande antilope d'Afrique. Elle habite les régions d'épineux ainsi que la brousse. C'est un animal qui se nourrit surtout de feuilles mais qui, à l'occasion, broutera des pousses d'herbe fraîche. Il vit en petites hardes mais forme de grands troupeaux à la saison des migrations. L'éland est un remarquable sauteur. La femelle met bas un seul petit après une gestation de neuf mois. Cette antilope peut vivre pendant 12 ans.

ELENANTILOPE

Sie ist die größte Antilope in Afrika. Ihr Habitat variiert von der Halbwüste und Buschsavanne bis zu Berggegenden. Sie sind Äser, fressen aber auch Graskeime. Sie bewegen sich in kleinen Herden, die sich aber während der Wanderschaft vergrößern. Elen sind ausgezeichnete Springer. Jeweils ein Kalb wird nach einer Tragzeit von neun Monaten geboren. Die Geburten nehmen während der Regenzeit zu. Die Lebenserwartung liegt bei 12 Jahren.

Taurotragus oryx

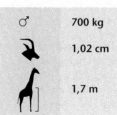 ♂ 700 kg

1,02 cm

1,7 m

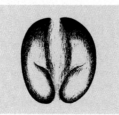

KRUGER, MARAKELE,
ADDO ELEPHANT,
AUGRABIES FALLS,
GOLDEN GATE HIGHLANDS,
KALAHARI GEMSBOK, ZUURBERG,
KAROO, \HEI-!GARIEP,
MOUNTAIN ZEBRA,
WEST COAST

Tragelaphus strepsiceros

KUDU

Kudu prefer wooded savanna and are fond of broken, rocky areas with water. They are browsers, and occur in groups of up to 12 animals. The alarm call is a deep bark. When they flee, the tail is curled up so that the white hair underneath it becomes visible. Kudu can clear a two-metre-high fence with ease. A single calf is born after a gestation period of seven months.

KOEDOE

Koedoes is blaarvreters wat 'n boomryke habitat verkies, en is lief vir gebroke, rotsagtige areas met water. Hulle is tropdiere, en kom voor in groepe van tot 12 diere. Hulle waarskuwingsroep is 'n diep blaf. Wanneer hulle weghardloop, krul hulle die stert op sodat dit wit vertoon. Hulle spring met gemak oor 'n heining van twee meter. 'n Enkele kalf word gebore na 'n draagtyd van sewe maande.

LE KOUDOU

Le koudou habite la savane arbustive et affectionne aussi les terrains accidentés à proximité des points d'eau. Il se nourrit de feuilles et vit en hardes d'une douzaine d'animaux. En cas d'alerte, il pousse un cri rauque. Quand il est en fuite, il soulève sa queue de façon à en exhiber la partie blanche. Le koudou franchit avec aisance une clôture de deux mètres. La femelle met bas un seul petit après une gestation de sept mois. Le koudou peut vivre pendant 11 ans.

KUDU

Kuduantilopen bevorzugen Baumsavanne und liebt felsiges Gelände mit Wasser. Diese Antilopen formieren sich zu Gruppen bis zu 12 Tieren und sind meist Äser. Kudus sind während der Nacht aktiv. Ihr Alarmruf ist ein tiefes Bellen. Auf der Flucht stellen sie den Schwanz auf. Kudus können mühelos über einen zwei Meter hohes Hinderniss springen. Nach sieben Monaten wird ein Kalb geboren. Die Lebenserwartung der Kudus liegt bei 11 Jahren.

Tragelaphus strepsiceros

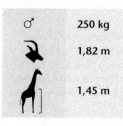

♂	250 kg
	1,82 m
	1,45 m

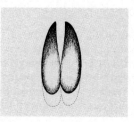

Kruger, Marakele,
Addo Elephant,
Augrabies Falls,
Mountain Zebra,
Kalahari Gemsbok,
Karoo, \Hei-!gariep,
Zuurberg, West Coast

Tragelaphus angasii

NYALA

Nyala prefer dense bush. They are abundant in the Pafuri area of the Kruger National Park, where they occur mainly in small groups of two or three animals, but sometimes form transient groups of up to 30. Their alarm call is a deep bark. Nyala live mainly on leaves, shoots, flowers and fruit. After a gestation period of seven months a single calf is born in thickets, where it is tended by the ewe.

NJALA

Njala's verkies digte bos, maar nie noodwendig oewerbos nie. Hulle is volop in die Pafuri-gebied in die Krugerwildtuin. Hulle kom meestal in klein groepies voor, maar kan soms tydelike groepe van tot 30 diere vorm. Hul waarskuwings-roep is 'n diep blaf. Njala's leef hoofsaaklik op blare, takkies, blomme en vrugte. 'n Enkele lam word in ruigtes gebore, waar die ooi dit versorg.

LE NYALA

Le nyala habite les régions de brousse dense. On en rencontre beaucoup dans la région de Pafuri au Parc Kruger où ils vivent en petites hardes de deux ou trois individus, bien qu'ils se rassemblent temporairement en groupes d'une trentaine d'animaux. En cas d'alerte, ils poussent un cri rauque. Le nyala se nourrit de feuilles, de fleurs et de fruits. Après une gestation de sept mois, la femelle met bas dans les taillis un seul petit. Le nyala peut vivre pendant huit ans.

TIEFLAND-NYALA

Die Nyalas bevorzugen Regionen mit dichtem Busch. Sie sind in der Pafurige-gend des Kruger Nationalparks zu finden. Sie formieren sich meist in kleinen Gruppen von nur zwei oder drei Tieren; vorübergehend auch bis zu 30 Tieren. Ihr Alarmruf ist ein tiefes Bellen. Sie leben von Blättern, Zweigen und Blumen sowie Früchten. Nach einer Tragzeit von sieben Monaten wird ein Kalb gebo-ren. Die Lebenserwartung der Nyala liegt bei neun Jahren.

Tragelaphus angasii

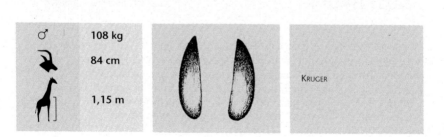

♂ 108 kg

84 cm

1,15 m

KRUGER

Tragelaphus scriptus

BUSHBUCK

Bushbuck prefer dense riverine bush. They are shy and solitary but also occur in small family groups. They are usually inactive by day but may be seen on cool days. The alarm call is a load, hoarse bark. Bushbuck are predominantly browsers but will feed on fresh green grass. A single young is born after a six-month gestation period. Life expectancy is nine years.

BOSBOK

Bosbokke verkies digte bosse langs riviere. Hulle is skugter en alleenlopend, maar kom ook in klein familiegroepe voor. Gewoonlik is hulle bedags onaktief, maar op koel dae kan hulle gesien word. Hul alarmroep is 'n skerp, diep blaf. Bosbokke is hoofsaaklik blaarvreters, maar sal sagte, groen gras ook vreet. 'n Enkele kleintjie word gebore na 'n draagtyd van ses maande.

LE GUIB HARNACHE

Cet animal habite les régions de brousse dense et à proximité des points d'eau. Bien qu'il soit surtout solitaire et craintif, on le rencontre aussi en petites hardes regroupant une famille. Il n'est généralement pas actif pendant la journée sauf quand il fait frais. En cas d'alerte, il pousse un cri rauque et enroué. Le guib harnaché se nourrit de feuilles mais aussi d'herbe fraîche. La femelle met bas un seul petit après une gestation de six mois. L'animal peut vivre pendant neuf ans.

BUSCHBOCK

Der Buschbock bevorzugt dichtbewachsene Flußläufe. Es sind scheue und ungesellige Antilopen, die man aber in kleinen, jedoch sehr lockeren Familiengruppen antreffen kann. Tagsüber ruhen sie meist, zeigen sich jedoch gegentlich an kühlen Tagen. Ihr Alarmruf ist ein lautes, heiseres Bellen. Sie sind Äser, fressen aber auch frisches Gras. Nach sechs Monaten wird ein Junges geboren. Die Lebenserwartung der Tiere liegt bei neun Jahren.

Tragelaphus scriptus

♂	45 kg	
	52 cm	
	80 cm	

MAJOR
ADDO ELEPHANT,
MOUNTAIN ZEBRA,
ZUURBERG
TSITSIKAMMA

Hippotragus equinus

ROAN ANTELOPE

This scarce antelope has a preference for open woodland with long grass and surface water. Both sexes have horns, but those of the females are thinner. Roan Antelope are essentially grazers but will browse. They are gregarious and live in groups of up to 12. Breeding herds comprise a dominant male; bachelor herds also occur. After a nine-month gestation period one calf is born.

BASTERGEMSBOK

'n Skaars boksoort, met 'n voorkeur vir oop savanna met lang gras en oppervlak-water. Hulle is tropdiere en leef in troppe van tot 12 diere. Teelgroepe met 'n dominante bul, asook vrygeselgroepe word gevind. Beide geslagte het horings, maar die koeie s'n is dunner. Bastergemsbokke is veral grasvreters, maar sal ook blare vreet. Een kalfie word na 'n draagtyd van nege maande gebore.

L'ANTILOPE CHEVAL

Antilope rare qui préfère la savane herbeuse et les régions avec de l'eau. Mâles et femelles ont tous les deux des cornes mais celles de la femelle sont plus fines. Cette antilope se nourrit principalement d'herbes. C'est un animal grégaire qui vit en groupes qui peuvent atteindre 12 individus. Il existe aussi des groupes dominés par un seul mâle. La femelle met bas un petit après une gestation de neuf mois. Cette espèce peut vivre pendant 19 ans.

PFERDEANTILOPE

Diese seltene Antilope bevorzugt offene Baumsavanne mit hohem Gras und Zugang zu Wasser. Beide Geschlechter haben Hörner, aber die des Weibchen sind kleiner. Gelegentlich äsen sie auch. Sie sind gesellige Tiere und leben in Gruppen bis zu 12 Antilopen. Herden werden von einem dominierenden Bullen angeführt, und die übrigen Männchen schließen sich zu Junggesellenherden zusammen. Ein Junges wird geboren. Die Lebenserwartung liegt bei 19 Jahren.

Hippotragus niger

SABLE ANTELOPE

Preferring open woodland with ample grass and water, Sable Antelope are mainly grazers. The older bulls are black while cows and younger bulls are brown. Both sexes have horns. Sable Antelope are gregarious and live in herds. Bulls are territorial and bachelor herds are formed by sub-dominant bulls. After a nine-month gestation period a single calf is born. Life expectancy is 19 years.

SWARTWITPENS

Swartwitpense verkies ylbeboste grasvlaktes met beskikbare water. Die ouer bulle is swart, terwyl die koeie en jonger bulle bruin is. Beide geslagte het horings. Hulle is sosiaal en kom voor in troppe. Bulle is territoriaal, en subdominante bulle vorm vrygeselgroepe. Swartwitpense vreet hoofsaaklik gras. 'n Enkele kalf word gebore na 'n draagtyd van nege maande.

L'HIPPOTRAGUE NOIR

L'hippotrague noir se nourrit essentiellement d'herbes et habite la savane herbeuse et arborée à proximité de l'eau. Les vieux mâles sont noirs tandis que les femelles et les jeunes mâles ont un pelage brun. Mâles et femelles ont tous les deux des cornes. C'est un animal grégaire qui vit en groupes comptant de 10 à 30 antilopes. Les mâles marquent leur territoire. La femelle met bas un petit après une gestation de neuf mois. Cette espèce peut vivre pendant 19 ans.

RAPPENANTILOPE

Es ist eine herrliche Antilope. Als grasfressende Tiere bevorzugen sie vor allem lichte Baumsavannen mit Wasserquellen. Die älteren Bullen sind schwarz, das Weibchen und der Jungbullen braun. Beide Geschlechter haben Hörner. Sie sind gesellig; Gruppen von 10 bis 30 Tieren sind nicht selten. Bullen beanspruchen ihre eigenen Gebiete. Nach neun Monaten wird ein Kalb geboren. Die Lebenserwartung der Antilopen liegt bei 19 Jahren.

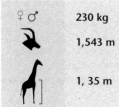 ♀ ♂   230 kg

1,543 m

1, 35 m

KRUGER

119

Oryx gazella

GEMSBOK

Adapted to survive in arid, waterless environments, Gemsbok live in groups of up to 12 animals but split into smaller groups during dry periods. They graze and browse, obtaining moisture from plants, especially roots and wild fruit such as tsamas. Bulls are territorial, marking their areas with dung middens. After a nine-month gestation period a single calf is born. Life expectancy is 19 years.

GEMSBOK

'n Woestyndier wat aangepas is vir 'n dorre, waterlose omgewing. Hulle leef in groepe van tot 12 diere, maar verdeel in kleiner groepe gedurende droë sei-soene. Bulle is territoriaal en merk hul gebiede met mishope. Hulle is gras- en blaarvreters, wat hul vog van plantvoedsel, veral plantwortels en vrugte soos tsamas, kry. 'n Enkele kalf word gebore na 'n draagtyd van nege maande.

L'ORYX

C'est un animal adapté aux régions arides et il peut survivre pendant longtemps sans eau. Il vit en petits groupes comprenant une douzaine d'animaux, et qui se subdivisent en petites hardes à la saison sèche. Il se nourrit d'herbes et de feuilles. Il extirpe l'humidité des plantes et particulièrement celle des racines et des fruits sauvages tel que le melon tsama. Le mâle marque son territoire de ses excréments. La femelle met bas un seul petit. L'oryx peut vivre pendant 19 ans.

ORYXANTILOPE

Diese Antilope hat sich an wasserloses, arides Gelände angepaßt und lebt in Gruppen bis zu zwölf Tieren. In Dürrezeiten verkleinern sich die Gruppen. Sie sind Grasfresser und Äser; sie erhalten Flüssigkeit über Pflanzen, über Wurzeln und Feldrüchte wie z.B. die 'Tsama'. Die Bullen markieren ihr Gebiet durch Exkremente. Nach neun Monaten wird ein Kalb geboren. Die Lebenserwartung der Tiere liegt bei 19 Jahren.

Oryx gazella

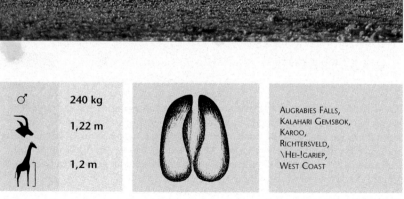

♂ 240 kg

1,22 m

1,2 m

AUGRABIES FALLS,
KALAHARI GEMSBOK,
KAROO,
RICHTERSVELD,
\HEI-!GARIEP,
WEST COAST

Kobus ellipsiprymnus

WATERBUCK

Waterbuck are characterized by a white ring around the rump. They are always found close to water, usually in mountainous terrain. Waterbuck are mainly grazers but will also browse. They are social and occur in groups of 12 to 30, with territorial bulls. After a nine-month gestation period the cows leave the group to give birth, in seclusion, to one or two young. Life expectancy is 12 years.

WATERBOK

Waterbokke word gekenmerk deur 'n wit kring om die stert. Hulle is altyd naby water en verkies dikwels bergagtige gebiede. Hulle is sosiaal, en kom voor in groepe van 12 tot 30 lede, met territoriale bulle. Waterbokke is hoofsaaklik grasvreters, maar sal ook blare vreet. Die koeie verlaat die trop om in afsondering geboorte te gee aan een of twee kleintjies na 'n draagtyd van nege maande.

LE COB A CROISSANT

Cette antilope se caractérise par un cercle blanc autour de la croupe. On la rencontre toujours à proximité de l'eau et dans les zones montagneuses. Le cob à croissant se nourrit d'herbes mais consomment des feuilles à l'occasion. Animal sociable, il vit en groupes comprenant de 12 à 30 animaux et que dirige un mâle dominant. Après une gestation de neuf mois, la femelle quitte le groupe pour mettre bas à l'écart un ou deux petits. Cet animal peut vivre pendant 12 ans.

WASSERBOCK

Diese Antilope lebt in Wassernähe in bergiger Umgebung. Sie ist durch einen weißen Ring am Hinterteil gekennzeichnet. Wasserböcke fressen Gras, äsen aber auch. Sie sind gesellig und formieren sich zu Gruppen von 12 bis 30 Tieren mit jeweils einem Leitbullen. Ist die Kuh trächtig, verläßt sie die Gruppe und verbringt die Zeit bis zur Geburt in Abgeschiedenheit. Sie gebärt ein oder zwei Junge. Die Lebenserwartung liegt bei 12 Jahren.

Kobus ellipsiprymnus

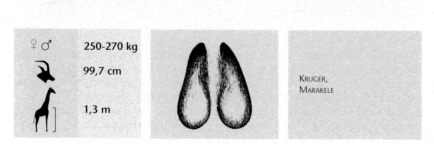

♀ ♂   **250-270 kg**

99,7 cm

1,3 m

KRUGER,
MARAKELE

123

Redunca fulvorufula

MOUNTAIN REEDBUCK

These animals occur on dry, grassy slopes with ample shrub or trees for shelter. They are grazers and are active mainly during the early morning and late afternoon. Mountain Reedbuck are found in groups of up to 30 animals. Dominant rams are territorial, while sub-dominant rams form bachelor groups. After an eight-month gestation period a single young is born and hidden in dense shelter.

ROOIRIBBOK

Hulle kom voor op droë, grasbedekte heuwels met genoeg struike of bome vir skuiling. Rooiribbokke kom voor in groepe van tot 30 diere. Dominante ramme is territoriaal, en sub-dominante ramme vorm vrygeselgroepe. Hulle is grasvreters, en is meestal aktief in die vroeë oggend en laatmiddag. Na 'n draagtyd van agt maande word een kleintjie gebore, wat dan in 'n digte skuiling wegkruip.

LE COB DES MONTAGNES

Le cob des montagnes habite les pentes sèches et herbeuses et là où il y a des broussailles et des arbres pour l'abriter. Actif le matin et en fin d'après-midi, il mange de l'herbe. On le rencontre en groupes qui peuvent compter jusqu'à une trentaine d'animaux. Le mâle dominant est territorial tandis que les autres mâles forment de petits groupes. Après une gestation de huit mois, la femelle met bas un petit qu'elle cache dans les fourrés. Cet animal peut vivre pendant huit ans.

BERGRIEDBOCK

Diese Tiere leben auf trockenen, grasigen Berghängen mit genügend Buschwerk oder Bäumen zu ihrem Schutz. Es sind grasfressende Tiere, meist morgens und nachmittags aktiv. Sie schließen sich zu Gruppen von ungefähr 30 Tieren zusammen. Die Böcke beanspruchen jeweils ihr eigenes Gebiet. Diejenigen, die kein eigenes Gebiet haben, formieren sich zu einer Herde. Nach acht Monaten wird ein Junges geboren. Ihre Lebenserwartung liegt bei acht Jahren.

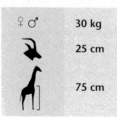

♀ ♂	30 kg
	25 cm
	75 cm

KRUGER,
MOUNTAIN ZEBRA,
GOLDEN GATE HIGHLANDS,
KAROO, MARAKELE

Redunca arundinum

REEDBUCK

Reedbuck occur in dense reed patches and grassy vleis close to rivers. The alarm call is a sharp whistle, and they display the white underside of the tail when fleeing. Reedbuck are found in pairs or family groups. While they are predominantly grazers, they will sometimes browse. After seven and a half months' gestation a single lamb is born and hidden in tall grass.

RIETBOK

Rietbokke kom voor in digbegroeide rietkolle en grasvleie naby riviere. Hul waarskuwingsroep is 'n skerp fluitgeluid. Die wit onderkant van hul stert wys wanneer hulle weghardloop. Rietbokke kom voor in pare of in familiegroepe. Hulle is oorwegend grasvreters, maar sal soms blare vreet. Na 'n draagtyd van sewe en 'n half maand word 'n enkele lam gebore en weggesteek in lang gras.

LE COB DES ROSEAUX

On le rencontre dans les zones marécageuses, dans les roseaux près des rivières. Quand il se sent menacé, il émet un sifflement strident et exhibe le blanc du dessous de sa queue lorsqu'il s'enfuie. Il vit en couple ou en groupe familial. Il se nourrit d'herbes, quoiqu'il lui arrive de brouter aussi des feuilles. Après une gestation de sept mois et demi, la femelle met bas un seul petit qu'elle cache dans les hautes herbes. Cette antilope peut vivre pendant neuf ans.

RIEDBOCK

Riedböcke leben im Röhricht und in grasbewachsenen Schwemmlandzonen in der Nähe von Flüssen. Ihr Alarmruf ist ein scharfes Flöten; auf der Flucht zeigen sie die weiße Unterseite des Schwanzes. Sie bewegen sich in Paaren oder Gruppen. Sie sind Grasfresser und Äser. Nach siebeneinhalb Monaten wird ein Junges geboren und für zwei bis drei Monate im hohem Gras versteckt. Die Lebenserwartung der Riedböcke liegt bei neun Jahren.

Redunca arundinum

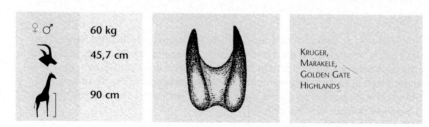

♀ ♂   60 kg

45,7 cm

90 cm

KRUGER,
MARAKELE,
GOLDEN GATE
HIGHLANDS

Pelea capreolus

GREY RHEBOK

Grey Rhebok are grazers and occur mainly on mountain slopes with good grass cover. They flee with a characteristic 'rocking-horse' motion, displaying the white underside of the tail. They live in small groups of up to 12 animals, and rams are territorial. After a gestation period of eight and a half months a single young is born, in November or December.

VAALRIBBOK

Die vaalribbok kom veral voor op berghange met goeie grasbedekking. Hulle vlug met 'n kenmerkende 'skommelperd-beweging' en wys die wit onderkant van die stert. Hulle leef in troppe van tot 12 diere. Die ramme is territoriaal. Vaalribbokke is uitsluitlik grasvreters. 'n Enkele lam word gedurende November of Desember gebore na 'n draagtyd van agt en 'n half maand.

LE RHEBOK GRIS

Le rhebok gris est une antilope gracieuse, qui se nourrit d'herbes et vit princi-palement sur les pentes herbeuses des montagnes. Lorsqu'il prend la fuite, l'animal saute d'une manière très caractéristique et exhibe la partie blanche sous sa queue. Il vit en petits groupes de 12 antilopes au maximum et le mâle est territorial. Après une période de gestation de huit mois et demi, la femelle met bas un seul petit en novembre ou décembre.

REHBOCK

Der Rehbock ist ein grasfressendes Tier. Es bevorzugt schöne Berghänge. Auf der Flucht bewegen sich die Tiere mit einer charakteristischen, schaukelpferd-artigen Bewegung und zeigen die weiße Unterseite ihres Schwanzes. Sie for-mieren sich in kleinen Gruppen; die Böcke beanspruchen jeweils ein eigenes Gebiet, das sie markieren. Nach achteinhalb Monaten wird ein Junges im November oder Dezember geboren.

Pelea capreolus

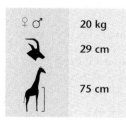

♀ ♂	20 kg
	29 cm
	75 cm

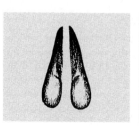

Kruger,
Mountain Zebra,
Bontebok,
Golden Gate Highlands,
Karoo, West Coast

129

Alcelaphus buselaphus

RED HARTEBEEST

A gregarious animal that prefers open grassland and sparse scrub, the Red Harte-beest is a grazer but will sometimes also browse. They occur in groups of 20 individuals, but occasionally herds number in the thousands. Males are territorial during the rut. After an eight-month gestation period a single calf is born; it is hidden in tall grass and suckled until strong enough to join the herd.

ROOIHARTEBEES

'n Tropdier wat vlaktewêreld en yl bosveld verkies. Hulle kom voor in troppe van tot 20 diere, maar soms vorm troppe van meer as 'n duisend. Die bulle is territoriaal tydens paartyd. Hulle is grasvreters, maar sal ook blare vreet. Na 'n draagtyd van agt maande gee koeie geboorte aan een kalf, wat in lang gras weg-gesteek en gevoed word, totdat dit sterk genoeg is om by die trop aan te sluit.

LE BUBALE ROUGE

C'est un animal grégaire qui vit dans la savane herbeuse. Le bubale rouge se nourrit d'herbes mais consomme parfois aussi des feuilles. Il vit en groupes d'une vingtaine d'animaux mais il arrive qu'on rencontre des troupeaux beau-coup plus nombreux. A la saison du rut, le mâle est territorial. Après une gesta-tion de huit mois, la femelle met bas un seul petit qu'elle cache et allaite dans les hautes herbes jusqu'à ce qu'il soit assez grand pour se joindre au troupeau.

KUHANTILOPE

Ein geselliges Tier, das offenes Grasland und spärliches Buschwerk liebt. Es ist eine grasfressende Antilope, die aber auch äst. Sie formieren sich zu Gruppen von 20 Mitgliedern, doch wachsen ihre Herden manchmal zu Tausenden an. Während der Brunftzeit grenzen die Bullen ihre Gebiete ab. Nach achtmona-tiger Tragzeit wird ein Junges geboren; es wird im Gras verborgen und dort gesäugt, bis es stark genug ist, sich der Herde anzuschließen.

Alcelaphus buselaphus

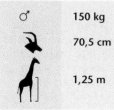

♂ 150 kg

70,5 cm

1,25 m

ADDO ELEPHANT, MARAKELE,
AUGRABIES FALLS,
MOUNTAIN ZEBRA,
GOLDEN GATE HIGHLANDS,
KALAHARI GEMSBOK, KAROO,
\HEI-!GARIEP, WEST COAST

Damaliscus lunatus

TSESSEBE

Considered the fastest antelope in southern Africa, Tsessebe prefer watered transitional zones between woodland and grassveld. They are grazers and are fond of new growth after a fire. Tsessebe occur in small groups, and bulls are territorial. After an eight-month gestation period a single calf is born, and can run soon after birth. Life expectancy is 20 years.

TSESSEBE

Die tsessebe is lief vir oorgangsgebiede tussen boomsavanna en grasveld, met beskikbare water. Hulle kom in klein troppe voor. Die bulle is territoriaal. Hulle is grasvreters en verkies nuwe groei na 'n veldbrand. Tsessebe's word beskou as die vinnigste boksoort in Suider-Afrika. Na 'n draagtyd van agt maande word 'n enkele kalf gebore, wat reeds kort na geboorte kan hardloop.

LE SASSABY

Considéré comme l'antilope la plus rapide d'Afrique australe, le sassaby habite les endroits où il y a de l'eau et spécialement dans les zones de transition entre la savane herbeuse et la savane boisée. Il se nourrit d'herbes et des plantes qui repoussent immédiatement après le feu. Il vit en petites hardes et le mâle est territorial. Après une gestation de huit mois, la femelle met bas un seul petit qui peut gambader peu après la naissance. Le sassaby peut vivre pendant 20 ans.

LEIERANTILOPE

Die Leierantilopen sind wahrscheinlich die schnellsten Antilopen in Afrika. Sie bevorzugen wasserreiche Übergangszonen von Grasland zu Baumsavannen. Sie lieben besonders das frische Gras nach einem Steppenbrand. Ihre Gruppen sind klein, und die Bullen grenzen ihr Gebiet, beziehungsweise das der Herde, ab. Nach einer achtmonatigen Tragzeit wird ein Junges geboren, das kurz nach der Geburt laufen kann. Die Lebenserwartung der Tiere liegt bei 20 Jahren.

Damaliscus lunatus

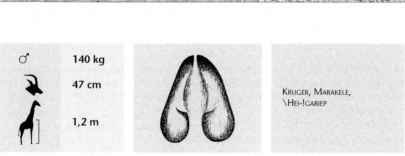

♂ 140 kg

47 cm

1,2 m

KRUGER, MARAKELE,
\HEI-!GARIEP

Damaliscus dorcas dorcas

BONTEBOK

Bontebok are indigenous to a restricted area of the southwestern Cape. They are closely related to the Blesbok but inhabit coastal plains with available water and shelter within the fynbos biome. Bontebok are grazers and prefer short grass. They are gregarious; bulls are territorial. After an eight-month gestation period a single calf is born, from September to November.

BONTEBOK

Die bontebok is inheems tot 'n beperkte gebied in die Suidwes-Kaap. Hulle is naverwant aan die blesbok, maar verkies kusvlaktes met water en skuiling, binne die fynbosbioom. Bontebokke is tropdiere en bulle is territoriaal. Hulle is grasvreters wat kort gras verkies. Na 'n draagtyd van agt maande word 'n enkele kalf vanaf September tot November gebore.

LE BONTEBOK

Ce damalisque à front blanc est originaire uniquement d'une petite région du sud-ouest de la province du Cap. Il est étroitement apparenté au blesbok mais on le trouve dans les plaines côtières bien arrosées et dans les zones de 'fynbos'. Le bontebok se nourrit d'herbes et en particulier d'herbes courtes. Il est grégaire et le mâle est territorial. Après une période de gestation de huit mois, la femelle met bas un seul petit entre septembre et novembre.

BUNTBOCK

Der gesellige Buntbock ist ein einheimisches Tier in einigen Gebieten am Südwestkap. Er ist eng mit dem Bleßbock verwandt, bevorzugt aber die Küstenebenen und sucht Zuflucht innerhalb des Fynbos-Bioms. Als Grasfresser lieben sie besonders kurze Gräser. Die Bullen haben ihre eigenen Gebiete, die sie von einander abgrenzen. Nach einer achtmonatigen Tragzeit wird zwischen September und November ein Junges geboren.

Damaliscus dorcas dorcas

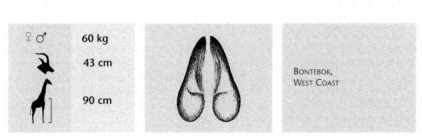

♀ ♂   60 kg

       43 cm

       90 cm

BONTEBOK,
WEST COAST

Damaliscus dorcas phillipsi

BLESBOK

The Blesbok is more common than the Bontebok and occurs from the Eastern Cape to the Transvaal. The white blaze on the forehead is divided in two, and the legs, belly and rump are not as white as those of the Bontebok. These grazers favour grassland with water and prefer short grass. A single lamb is born, usually during December, after a gestation period of eight months.

BLESBOK

Die blesbok is meer algemeen as die bontebok, en kom voor op die Hoëveld wat strek van die Oos-Kaap tot die Transvaal. Die bles op die voorkop is in twee verdeel, en die bene, pens en kruis is nie so wit soos die bontebok s'n nie. Hierdie grasvreters se voorkeurhabitat is grasveld met kort gras en beskikbare water. Een lam word tydens Desember gebore na 'n draagtyd van agt maande.

LE BLESBOK

Moins rare que le bontebok, le blesbok a une aire de répartition plus vaste qui s'étend du Cap oriental jusqu'au Transvaal. La marque blanche sur son front se divise en deux segments et ses pattes, son ventre et sa croupe ne sont pas aussi blancs que ceux du bontebok. Il vit dans les régions où il y a de l'eau et des herbes courtes. Après une gestation de huit mois, la femelle met bas un seul petit, généralement en décembre.

BLEßBOCK

Diese Antilope ist weiter verbreitet als der Buntbock. Ihr Lebensraum erstreckt sich vom Ostkap bis ins Transvaal. Ihre weiße Blesse auf der Stirn ist unterbrochen, und das Fell an Beinen, am Bauch und Hinterteil ist nicht so weiß wie das des Buntbocks. Es sind grasfressende Antilopen, die Zugang zu Wasser benötigen. Jeweils ein Junges wird nach einer Tragzeit von acht Monaten geboren, normalerweise im September oder Oktober.

Damaliscus dorcas phillipsi

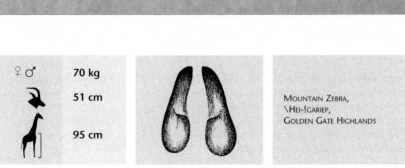

♀ ♂   70 kg

51 cm

95 cm

MOUNTAIN ZEBRA,
\HEI-!GARIEP,
GOLDEN GATE HIGHLANDS

137

Aepyceros melampus

IMPALA

Impala are common antelope in the bushveld regions. These antelope are gregarious and occur in groups of 20 to 100. They browse and graze. They can leap a distance of ten metres, clearing a height of three metres. Rams are territorial and very active during mating (April to May). Sub-dominant rams form bachelor herds. After a six-and-a-half-month gestation period a single lamb is born.

ROOIBOK

Die rooibok is die algemeenste boksoort in die bosveldstreke. Hulle is tropdiere en kom voor in groepe van 20 tot 100. Ramme is territoriaal en baie aktief tydens paartyd (April tot Mei). Sub-dominante ramme vorm vrygeseltroppe. Hulle is gras- en blaarvreters. Hulle kan tot tien meter ver en drie meter hoog spring. 'n Enkele lam word na 'n draagtyd van ses en 'n half maand gebore.

L'IMPALA

L'impala est l'antilope qu'on aperçoit le plus souvent dans le bushveld. C'est un animal grégaire qui vit en troupeaux qui peuvent compter de 20 à 100 animaux. L'impala se nourrit d'herbes et de feuilles. Son saut prodigieux peut atteindre dix mètres de largeur et trois de hauteur. Le mâle est territorial et très actif à l'époque du rut (d'avril à mai). Les autres mâles forment de petits groupes. Après une gestation de six mois et demi, la femelle met bas un seul petit.

IMPALA

Impala sind gesellige Antilopen, die in Buschsavannen häufig vorkommen. Sie formieren sich zu Gruppen von 20 bis 100 Tieren. Impalas äsen und weiden. Sie können zehn Meter weit und drei Meter hoch springen. Die Böcke sind während der Brunftzeit (April bis Mai) sehr aktiv. Potentielle Leittiere suchen sich Reviere, leben aber ansonsten in Junggesellenherden. Im November und Dezember werden die Kälber geboren.

Aepyceros melampus

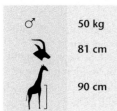

♂ 50 kg

81 cm

90 cm

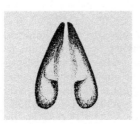

MARAKELE,
KRUGER

139

Antidorcas marsupialis

SPRINGBOK

Springbok are found in the drier western areas. They are gregarious, and herds number in the thousands when moving to new feeding grounds. When threatened, they 'pronk', bounding with the back arched and legs stiff. They are grazers and browsers. Rams are territorial during mating; sub-dominant rams form bachelor herds. After a five-and-a-half-month gestation period a single lamb is born.

SPRINGBOK

Springbokke kom in die droër, westelike dele voor. Hulle is sosiale diere wat in troppe van tot 100 voorkom. Ramme is territoriaal tydens paartyd, en sub-dominante ramme vorm vrygeseltroppe. Hulle is blaar- en grasvreters. Wanneer hulle bedreig word, 'pronk' hulle deur te draf-spring met 'n geboë rug en stywe bene. 'n Enkele lam word gebore na 'n draagtyd van vyf en 'n half maand.

LE SPRINGBOK

Le springbok vit dans les régions plus arides de l'ouest du pays. C'est un animal grégaire qui vit en troupeaux qui peuvent compter des milliers d'animaux lors des migrations saisonnières. Quand il se sent menacé, il 'pronk' (saut caractéristique du springbok). Il se nourrit d'herbes et de feuilles. Le mâle dominant est territorial à l'époque du rut et les autres mâles forment de petits groupes. Après une gestation de cinq mois et demi, la femelle met bas en été un seul petit.

SPRINGBOCK

Springböcke werden in den dürreren,westlichen Regionen angetroffen. Es sind sehr gesellige Tiere. Ihre Herden zählen Tausende, wenn sie zu neuen Weidegründen wandern. Bei Gefahr vollziehen sie Prellsprünge, indem sie mit gewölbtem Rücken und steifen Beine hoch in die Luft schnellen. Sie weiden und äsen. Potentielle Leittiere formen Junggesellenherden. Nach fünfeinhalb Monaten wird ein Junges geboren. Ihre Lebenserwartung liegt bei zehn Jahren.

Antidorcas marsupialis

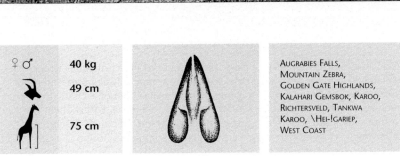

♀ ♂   **40 kg**

49 cm

75 cm

Augrabies Falls,
Mountain Zebra,
Golden Gate Highlands,
Kalahari Gemsbok, Karoo,
Richtersveld, Tankwa
Karoo, \Hei-!gariep,
West Coast

Neotragus moschatus

SUNI

Suni are found only in the north of the Kruger National Park, where they prefer dry woodland with dense undergrowth. They are usually solitary but also occur in small family groups. They are shy and wary, and live mainly by browsing on low shrubs, and also take wild fruit and mushrooms. After a gestation period of six months one young is born, during summer.

SOENIE

Soenies word net in die noorde van die Krugerwildtuin aangetref, waar hulle droë boomsavanna met digte onderbos verkies. Hulle is alleenlopend, maar kom ook in klein familiegroepe voor. Hulle is baie skugter en waaksaam, en leef hoofsaaklik van die blare van lae struike, asook veldvrugte en sampioene. Een kleintjie word in die somer gebore na 'n draagtyd van ses maande.

LE SUNI

C'est une antilope au pelage rouge brun. On la trouve dans la région nord du Parc Kruger, zone boisée et sèche avec d'abondantes broussailles. Animal habituellement solitaire, cette antilope vit en petit groupe familial. Le suni est craintif et aux aguets. Il se nourrit principalement de broussailles, de fruits sauvages et de champignons. Après une gestation de six mois, la femelle met bas en été un seul petit.

MOSCHUSBOCK

Das Fell dieser Antilope ist fuchsrot. Sie kommt nur im Norden des Kruger Nationalparks vor. Sie bevorzugt trockene Baumsavanne mit dichtem Unterholz. Normalerweise ist sie ein Einzelgänger, manchmal schließen sich die Tiere aber auch zu Gruppen zusammen. Ein Männchen hat ein bis vier Weibchen. Die Tiere sind scheu und wachsam. Sie äsen Blätter, fressen aber auch Früchte und Pilze. Nach sechs Monaten wird ein Junges im Sommer geboren.

♀♂   5 kg

13 cm

35 cm

KRUGER

Oreotragus oreotragus

KLIPSPRINGER

Klipspringers occur on rocky outcrops and in mountainous areas. Their specialized hooves enable them to bound up and down smooth boulders. The hair is hollow and spine-like, protecting them from extreme cold and heat. Klipspringers are very territorial and occur in pairs or small family groups. One young is born after a gestation period of seven months.

KLIPSPRINGER

Kom voor op klipkoppies en in bergagtige dele. Hul hoewe is aangepas om rats oor gladde rotse te kan beweeg. Hul hare is hol pennetjies wat as isolasie dien in baie koue en warm toestande. Klipspringers is baie territoriaal, en kom voor in pare of klein familiegroepe. Hulle leef van blare en veldvrugte. Na 'n draagtyd van sewe maande word 'n enkele kleintjie in 'n rotsskuiling gebore.

L'OREOTRAGUE

On rencontre cette antilope dans les régions montagneuses et sur les affleurements rocheux. L'oréotrague a des sabots spéciaux qui lui permettent de sauter sur les rochers lisses. Son pelage est formé de poils creux et rêches ce qui le protège des températures extrêmes. Il se nourrit de feuilles et de fruits sauvages. C'est un animal territorial qui vit en couple ou en petit groupe familial. Après une gestation de sept mois, la femelle met bas un petit dans un abri rocheux.

KLIPPSPRINGER

Klippspringer trifft man in felsigem oder bergigem Gelände an. Ihre charakteristischen Hufe ermöglichen es ihnen, gewandt von Fels zu Fels zu springen. Die dornenförmigen Fellhaare schützen sie vor extremer Kälte und Hitze. Sie äsen und leben von Wildfrüchten. Klippspringer leben meist in Paaren, gelegentlich bilden sie auch kleine Gruppen. Das männliche Tier verteidigt das Revier. Ein Junges wird nach sieben Monaten geboren.

Oreotragus oreotragus

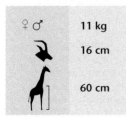

♀ ♂   **11 kg**

16 cm

60 cm

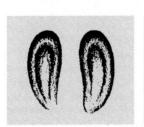

Kruger, Marakele,
Augrabies Falls, Karoo,
Mountain Zebra

Raphicerus campestris

STEENBOK

Widespread in a variety of habitats, Steenbok prefer open grassveld with sufficient shelter. They are selective grazers and browsers. Steenbok are solitary,
except during mating or when a lamb is present. They are territorial, and both
sexes mark and defend their territory. A single lamb is born after a five-and-a-
half-month gestation period.

STEENBOK

Steenbokke kom wydverspreid voor in 'n verskeidenheid habitatte. Hulle verkies oop grasveld met redelike skuiling. Hulle is alleenlopend, behalwe tydens
paarseisoen of wanneer daar 'n lam is. Steenbokke is territoriaal; beide geslagte
merk en verdedig hul territorium aktief. Hulle is selektiewe gras- en blaarvreters.
'n Enkele lammetjie word gebore na 'n draagtyd van vyf en 'n half maand.

LE STEENBOK

Très répandu dans divers habitats, le steenbok vit dans la savane herbeuse où il
peut se cacher. L'animal se nourrit en sélectionnant certaines herbes et feuilles.
C'est un animal solitaire, excepté à la saison de l'accouplement ou quand il y a
un petit. Le steenbok est très territorial: mâle et femelle marquent et défendent
leur territoire. Après une période de gestation de cinq mois et demi, la femelle
met bas un seul petit.

STEINBOCK

Der Steinbock ist in vielen Habitaten anzutreffen, bevorzugt aber offene Gegenden mit ausreichender Deckung. Sie sind sorgfältige Äser. Steinböcke sind
Einzelgänger – mit Ausnahme der Brunftzeit oder wenn sie Junge haben.
Beide Geschlechter beanspruchen ein eigenes Gebiet und markieren und
verteidigen dies auch. Auffallend ist, daß sie ihren Kot verscharren. Nach
einer Tragzeit von fünfeinhalb Monaten wird ein Junges geboren.

Raphicerus campestris

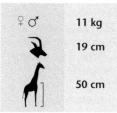 ♀ ♂

11 kg

19 cm

50 cm

Kruger, Marakele, Addo Elephant, Augrabies Falls, Mountain Zebra, Bontebok, Golden Gate Highlands, Kalahari Gemsbok, Zuurberg, Karoo, Richtersveld, Tankwa Karoo, \Hei-!Gariep, West Coast

Ourebia ourebi

ORIBI

These elegant antelope are threatened due to the contraction of their preferred habitat of open grassveld or flood plains with long grass offering ample shelter. They are mainly grazers but will take small amounts of browse. Usually solitary, they can occur in small groups of up to 12 animals. After a seven-month gestation period a single lamb is born, usually during summer.

OORBIETJIE

Die elegante oorbietjies word bedreig weens die inkrimping van hul habitat. Hulle verkies oop grasvelde of vloedvlaktes met lang gras wat goeie skuiling bied. Hulle is hoofsaaklik grasvreters wat min blare sal vreet. Hoewel hulle alleenlopend is, kom hulle voor in groepies van soveel as 12 diere. 'n Enkele lam word gewoonlik in die somer gebore na 'n draagtyd van sewe maande.

L'OUREBI

Cette gracieuse antilope est une espèce menacée à cause de la diminution progressive de son habitat préféré: les vastes étendues de savane herbeuse et les plaines fluviales aux hautes herbes protectrices. L'ourébi se nourrit principalement d'herbes mais consomme aussi des feuilles en petite quantité. Habituellement solitaire, il arrive qu'on le rencontre en petits groupes de 12 individus au maximum. Après une gestation de sept mois, la femelle met bas un seul petit.

BLEICHBOCK

Das Überleben dieser eleganten Antilope ist gefährdet, da ihr Habitat am Schwinden ist: Offene Grassavannen oder Schwemmlandgegenden mit hohem Gras für gute Deckung. Es sind fast ausschließlich grasende Tiere, aber sie äsen gelegentlich auch. Sie sind meist Einzelgänger, formieren aber auch kleine Herden bis zu zwölf Tieren. Ein Junges wird nach sieben Monaten Tragzeit geboren. Die Lebenserwartung eines Bleichbocks liegt bei 13 Jahren.

Ourebia ourebi

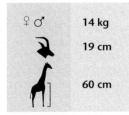

♀ ♂   14 kg

19 cm

60 cm

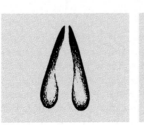

KRUGER,
GOLDEN GATE HIGHLANDS

Raphicerus melanotis

CAPE GRYSBOK

Cape Grysbok are usually solitary but may also occur in pairs. Mainly nocturnal, they are also active in the early morning and late afternoon. Although they prefer grazing, they also eat leaves and wild fruit. They are found mainly in dense shrub, ranging from mountainous areas to coastal forest. After a gestation period of six months a single lamb is born, during spring.

GRYSBOK

Grysbokke is alleenlopend of kom in pare voor. Hoewel hulle grasvreters is, sal hulle ook blare en veldvrugte vreet. Hulle word hoofsaaklik in digte struikbos gevind, van berggebiede tot by die kuswoude. Hoofsaaklik naglewend, maar ook aktief soggens en in die laatmiddag. 'n Enkele lam word in die lente gebore na 'n draagtyd van ses maande.

LE GRYSBOK DU CAP

Son pelage rouge brun est émaillé de poils gris. Le grysbok du Cap est habituellement solitaire mais il arrive qu'on l'aperçoive en couple. Il se nourrit surtout d'herbes mais aussi de feuilles et de fruits sauvages. Il vit principalement dans les régions broussailleuses en montagne tout comme dans les forêts côtières. Après une période de gestation de six mois, la femelle met bas un seul petit, généralement au printemps.

KAPGREISBOCK

Das Fell ist rötlichbraun und mit weißlichen Tupfen gesprenkelt. Das Männchen hat kurze, glatte und nach hinten gerichtete Hörner. Der Kapgreisbock ist meist ein Einzelgänger; die Tiere treten aber auch in Paaren auf. Er frißt Gras, Blätter und Wildfrüchte. Kapgreisböcke kommen in dichtbewachsenen Berggegenden und Küstengebieten vor. Sie sind überwiegend nachts aktiv. Nach einer Tragzeit von sechs Monaten wird ein Lamm im Frühjahr geboren.

Raphicerus melanotis

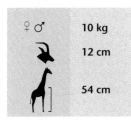

♀♂ 10 kg

12 cm

54 cm

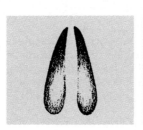

ADDO ELEPHANT,
BONTEBOK,
TSITSIKAMMA,
WEST COAST,
WILDERNESS

151

Raphicerus sharpei

SHARPE'S GRYSBOK

Sharpe's Grysbok occur in savanna regions with grass and shrubs of medium height, often preferring the rocky areas around koppies. They are nocturnal and shy, and seldom seen. They are mainly browsers but also take grass. Usually solitary, they sometimes occur in pairs; ewes and lambs are seen together. After a gestation period of six months one lamb is born.

SHARPE SE GRYSBOK

Kom voor in savannagebiede met mediumhoogte gras en struike. Hulle verkies ook klipperige gebiede rondom koppies. Hulle is naglewend en skugter, en dus moeilik om te sien. Alleenlopend, hoewel hulle in pare voorkom. Ooie en lammers word ook saam gesien. Hulle is hoofsaaklik blaarvreters, maar vreet ook gras. Een lam word gebore na 'n draagtyd van ses maande.

LE GRYSBOK DE SHARPE

Cette espèce d'animal habite les régions de savane herbeuse et broussailleuse et se tient de préférence dans les coins rocailleux et là où il y a de petites collines. Nocturne et craintif, c'est un animal qu'on aperçoit rarement. Le grysbok de Sharpe se nourrit d'herbes et parfois de feuilles aussi. Habituellement solitaire, on le rencontre quelquefois en couple. Après une gestation de six mois, la femelle ne met bas qu'un seul petit.

SHARPES GREISBOCK

Diese Antilopen kommen in Savannen mit Gras und Dickicht vor; sie bevorzugen felsige und hügelige Gegenden. Sie sind nachts aktiv und sehr scheu; man sieht sie selten. Sie sind meist Äser, fressen aber auch Gras. Obwohl sie Einzelgänger sind, kommen sie auch manchmal paarweise vor. Muttertier und Lamm werden zum Beispiel immer zusammen gesehen. Nach sechsmonatiger Tragzeit wird ein Lamm geboren.

Raphicerus sharpei

♀ ♂   7,5 kg

10 cm

45 cm

KRUGER

153

Cephalophus natalensis

RED DUIKER

Red Duiker are reddish brown in colour with slightly lighter underparts. They are found in thickly wooded areas close to water. They are browsers, but will also take wild fruit and seed pods. They are solitary; males are territorial. There is no fixed mating season and a single lamb is born at any time of the year but there is a birth peak during summer. Life expectancy is nine years.

ROOIDUIKER

Die rooiduiker is rooibruin van kleur met ligter onderdele. Hulle word in bosryke streke naby water aangetref. Hulle is alleenlopers; die rammetjies is territoriaal. Rooiduikers is blaarvreters, maar sal ook veldvrugte en saadpeule vreet. Daar is geen vaste paartyd nie, en 'n enkele lam word veral gedurende die somer gebore. Hul waarskynlike lewensduur is nege jaar.

LE CEPHALOPHE A FLANCS ROUX

Cette antilope au pelage roux, légèrement plus clair sur la partie inférieure de son corps, vit dans les endroits très broussailleux et à proximité des points d'eau. Le céphalophe à flancs roux consomment des feuilles, des fruits sauvages et des gousses de graines. Il est solitaire et le mâle est territorial. Il n'a pas de période de reproduction fixe et la femelle met bas un seul petit. Ce céphalophe peut vivre pendant neuf ans.

ROTDUCKER

Das Fell des Rotducker ist kastanienfarben, mit etwas helleren Tönen am Bauch. Die Tiere sind Einzelgänger und bevorzugen dichtbewachsene Waldgebiete in Wassernähe. Rotducker äsen, fressen aber auch Wildfrüchte und Keime. Die Bullen markieren ihre jeweiligen Gebiete. Es gibt keine bestimmte Brunftzeit. Lämmer werden das gesamte Jahr über gezeugt. Die Lebenserwartung der Rotducker liegt bei neun Jahren.

Cephalophus natalensis

♀ ♂   14 kg

            10 cm

            43 cm

KRUGER

Philantomba monticola

BLUE DUIKER

The smallest South African antelope, the Blue Duiker occurs in the dense forests of the south and east coasts. It is not easily seen and approaches open areas with caution. They are browsers, selecting accessible parts of the lower underbrush. Normally solitary, they temporarily associate in pairs. A single lamb is born after a gestation period of about five months. Life expectancy is nine years.

BLOUDUIKER

Die Blouduiker is die kleinste van ons antilope, en word in digte woude aan die suid- en ooskus gevind. Hulle is gewoonlik alleenlopend, maar kom tydelik voor in pare. Dit is moeilik om hulle waar te neem, omdat hulle oop gebiede baie versigtig benader. Blouduikers vreet blare, maar verkies plantdele van die onderbos. 'n Enkele lam word gebore. Hul waarskynlike lewensduur is nege jaar.

LE CEPHALOPHE BLEU

C'est la plus petite des antilopes d'Afrique du Sud. On la trouve dans les régions de forêt dense du sud et de l'est du pays. C'est un animal très craintif et il est rare qu'on l'aperçoive. Le céphalophe bleu se nourrit de feuillages et choisit les feuilles les plus basses qui lui sont les plus accessibles. En général solitaire, il vit en couple de façon temporaire. Après une gestation de cinq mois, la femelle met bas un seul petit. Cette espèce peut vivre pendant neuf ans.

BLAUDUCKER

Der Blauducker ist die kleinste südafrikanische Antilope. Er bevorzugt die dichten Wäldern der Süd- und Ostküste. Er ist schwer zu erblicken, und er nähert sich offenem Gelände nur mit großer Vorsicht. Die Blauducker sind Äser und suchen sich die unteren Teile der Büsche und des Gestrüpps aus, um daran zu nagen. Jeweils ein Lamm wird nach ungefähr fünf Monaten geboren. Die Lebenserwartung der Tiere liegt bei neun Jahren.

Philantomba monticola

♀ ♂ 4 kg

6 cm

30 cm

Tsitsikamma

Sylvicapra grimmia

COMMON DUIKER

Probably the most common antelope in Africa, Common Duikers prefer fairly dense bush with sufficient undergrowth. They are browsers, utilizing leaves and shoots, also taking flowers and fruits, and often digging for roots or tubers. Normally solitary, they associate in pairs during mating. After a three-month gestation period a single young is born and hidden in cover; it can run within 24 hours.

GEWONE DUIKER

Waarskynlik die algemeenste antiloop in Afrika. Hulle verkies redelik digte veld met voldoende skuiling. Hulle is blaarvreters wat ook lote, blomme en vrugte vreet. Grawe dikwels knolle en wortels uit. Gewoonlik alleenlopend, maar assosieer in pare tydens paarseisoen. 'n Enkele kleintjie word goed weggesteek na geboorte, maar kan binne 24 uur hardloop. Die draagtyd duur drie maande.

LE CEPHALOPHE COMMUN

C'est l'antilope la plus commune d'Afrique. Elle habite là où il y a d'épaisses broussailles pour l'abriter. Cet animal consomme des feuilles, de jeunes pousses, des fruits et a tendance à creuser pour déterrer des racines et des tubercules. En général solitaire, il s'accouple à la saison de la reproduction. Après une gestation de trois mois, la femelle met bas un petit qu'elle cache dans les fourrés mais qui est prêt à gambader dans les 24 heures. L'animal peut vivre pendant neuf ans.

KRONENDUCKER

Wahrscheinlich ist der Kronenducker die weitverbreiteste Antilopenart auf dem afrikanischen Kontinent. Die Tiere bevorzugen vor allem dichten Busch mit ausreichendem Unterholz. Es sind Äser; sie fressen Blätter, Blumen und Früchte. Oft graben sie nach Wurzeln oder Knollen. Nach drei Monaten wird ein Junges geboren und tief im Dickicht verborgen; es kann innerhalb von 24 Stunden laufen. Ihre Lebenserwartung liegt bei neun Jahren.

Sylvicapra grimmia

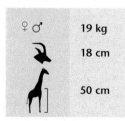

♀ ♂   19 kg

18 cm

50 cm

KRUGER, MARAKELE,
ADDO ELEPHANT, AUGRABIES
FALLS, MOUNTAIN ZEBRA,
BONTEBOK, KALAHARI
GEMSBOK, ZUURBERG,
KAROO, RICHTERSVELD,
TANKWA KAROO,
\HEI-!GARIEP, WEST COAST

INDEX